Witchcraft Trials

Fear, Betrayal, and Death in Salem

Other titles in the America's Living History series:

Alamo
Victory or Death on the Texas Frontier

ISBN-13: 978-0-7660-2937-8
ISBN-10:   0-7660-2937-9

Cuban Missile Crisis
In the Shadow of Nuclear War

ISBN-13: 978-0-7660-2905-7
ISBN-10:   0-7660-2905-0

The Fascinating History of American Indians
The Age Before Columbus

ISBN-13: 978-0-7660-2938-5
ISBN-10:   0-7660-2938-7

The Harlem Renaissance
An Explosion of African-American Culture

ISBN-13: 978-0-7660-2907-1
ISBN-10:   0-7660-2907-7

Space Race
The Mission, the Men, the Moon

ISBN-13: 978-0-7660-2910-1
ISBN-10:   0-7660-2910-7

Teetotalers and Saloon Smashers
The Temperance Movement and Prohibition

ISBN-13: 978-0-7660-2908-8
ISBN-10:   0-7660-2908-5

Women Win the Vote
The Hard-Fought Battle for Women's Suffrage

ISBN-13: 978-0-7660-2940-8
ISBN-10:   0-7660-2940-9

Witchcraft Trials

Fear, Betrayal, and Death in Salem

 Enslow Publishers, Inc.
40 Industrial Road
Box 398
Berkeley Heights, NJ 07922
USA
http://www.enslow.com

Deborah Kent

Library of Congress Cataloging-in-Publication Data:

Kent, Deborah.

Witchcraft trials: fear, betrayal, and death in Salem / Deborah Kent.

p. cm.—(America's living history)

Summary: "Examines the witchcraft hysteria in Salem Village in 1692, including the history of witchcraft, the principal participants in the accusations, the trials and judgment, and its legacy in American history"—Provided by publisher.

Includes bibliographical references and index.

ISBN-13: 978-0-7660-2906-4 (alk. paper)

ISBN-10: 0-7660-2906-9 (alk. paper)

1. Trials (Witchcraft)—Massachusetts—Salem—History—17th century—Juvenile literature. 2. Witchcraft—Massachusetts—Salem—History—17th century—Juvenile literature. 3. Salem (Mass.)—History—Colonial period, ca. 1600-1775—Juvenile literature. 4. Witchcraft—History—Juvenile literature. I. Title.

KFM2478.8.W5K456 2009

133.4'3097445—dc22

2008018393

Printed in the United States of America

10 9 8 7 6 5 4 3 2 1

To Our Readers: We have done our best to make sure all Internet Addresses in this book were active and appropriate when we went to press. However, the author and the publisher have no control over and assume no liability for the material available on those Internet sites or on other Web sites they may link to. Any comments or suggestions can be sent by e-mail to comments@enslow.com or to the address on the back cover.

♻ Enslow Publishers, Inc., is committed to printing our books on recycled paper. The paper in every book contains 10% to 30% post-consumer waste (PCW). The cover board on the outside of each book contains 100% PCW. Our goal is to do our part to help young people and the environment too!

Illustration Credits: The Art Archive/Culver Pictures, p. 55; Bridgeman Art Library, p. 9; Courtesy of bunkosquad via Flickr, p. 109 (top); Courtesy of Deaf RED Bear via Flickr, p. 109 (bottom); Enslow Publishers, Inc., pp. 38–39; The Everett Collection, p. 108; The Granger Collection, New York, pp. 6, 21, 28, 32, 83, 93; Harvard University Art Museum, p. 69; Photography by Joseph R. Modugno, p. 78; © Jupiterimages Corporation, pp. 27, 104; Library of Congress, pp. 49, 89, 100, 111–128; © North Wind Picture Archives, pp. 14, 63, 98; Courtesy of the Peabody Essex Museum, pp. 3, 25, 48, 59, 72, 81; Public domain image via Wikipedia.org, p. 54; Courtesy of Sandypaws via Flickr, p. 41; University of Virginia Library Special Collections, © The Rector and Visitors of the University of Virginia, 1999, p. 91.

Cover Illustration: The Granger Collection, New York (people praying for a girl allegedly afflicted by witchcraft).

Contents

A man tries to deliver a young woman from witchcraft by prayer in Salem, Massachusetts. The paranoia over witchcraft in the tiny village all began with a few girls trying to tell their fortunes.

DELIVERANCE FROM WITCHCRAFT BY PRAYER.

Chapter 1

The winter of 1692 was cold and long in Salem Village, Massachusetts. Nine-year-old Betty Parris and her cousin, eleven-year-old Abigail Williams, spent their evenings in their kitchen. They huddled close to the fire's warmth.

It was easy to feel lonely in Salem Village. The village was a collection of scattered farms amid trackless woods. The tavern and the church, or meetinghouse, were the only places where people could gather. Officially, Salem Village was part of Salem Town, seven miles away. Yet the village and the town had little in common. Salem Town was a busy seaport. Ships brought goods and news from Europe and the West Indies. Tucked away in the woods, Salem Village was separated from the town by a two-hour journey on horseback. After a heavy snow, the trip was almost impossible.

The parsonage was a four-room cottage where the village's minister lived. It had a small attached shed at the back. The reverend, Samuel Parris, lived there with his sickly wife, Elizabeth, their three children, and Parris's orphaned niece, Abigail. In addition, the Parris family had two live-in servants, a couple named Tituba and John Indian, who were slaves. The Reverend Parris had bought them on the Caribbean island of Barbados, where he

Slavery in Colonial Massachusetts

Slavery was permitted in Massachusetts, but it was not common. Historians estimate that about two hundred enslaved persons of African descent lived in the colony in 1690. Some American Indians were also held in slavery.[1]

Almost nothing is known of Tituba's background. Her name suggests to some historians that she may have belonged to the Yoruba people of West Africa.[2] Yet records about slaves brought into Massachusetts colony indicate that she and her husband, John, were Arawak Indians, originally from South America.

lived for several years before settling in Massachusetts.

Betty and Abigail had few toys or games to entertain them. The Reverend Parris was the minister of the village's meetinghouse. He and other Puritans strongly disapproved of idleness. He was convinced that fairy tales and games of make-believe were invitations from the devil. The only books in the house were the Bible and a collection of sermons.

Reverend Parris taught the children under his care to fear God almost as much as Satan. Despite their strict upbringing, however, Betty Parris and Abigail Williams broke the rules now and then.

Sometimes a girl from a neighboring farm dropped by for a visit on a winter evening. Betty and Abigail probably welcomed the company and the break in their routine. When one of their friends stopped in, the girls tried fortune-telling. Fortune-telling had become a popular, though secret, pastime in many New England villages. Cotton Mather, a leading Boston preacher of the day, wrote that many young people tried "conjuration with sieves and keys, and peas, and nails, and horseshoes."[3] Mather and other preachers warned that fortune-telling was sinful, a temptation from the devil. Nevertheless, right in the Reverend Parris's kitchen, young girls tried to forecast the future.

The girls chose a very simple fortune-telling method. One girl broke an egg and dropped the white into a glass of water. She carefully studied the pattern that the egg white formed as it drifted and spread. The pattern was supposed to give her a clue as to her future husband.

The girls of Salem Village must have thought the fortune-telling game was daring and dangerous. They knew that the Reverend Parris would be furious if he found out what they were doing. And suppose, as they had been warned, the devil noticed their game? Suppose he seized the chance and crept in to make his dreadful mischief?

Perhaps these thoughts made the fortune-telling game all the more exciting for some of the girls. For others, however, the

The Reverend Samuel Parris would have been angry if he knew that the girls were fortune-telling.

worry and fear may have been almost unbearable. One fateful evening, the floating egg white took a strange new form. Its strands twisted into sharp angles, and one of the girls said it looked like a coffin.[4] Surely this was a sign that they had gone too far. They thought evil was afoot due to their disobedience.

Trouble began soon after the frightening night when the coffin shape appeared. Sometime in January 1692, Betty Parris began to act strangely. Soon Abigail, too, behaved in a way no one could understand. John Hale, pastor in the nearby town of Beverly, described the girls' behavior. He reported that they mystified the household "by getting into holes, and creeping under chairs and stools, and [using] sturdy odd postures and antic gestures, uttering foolish, ridiculous speeches, which neither they themselves nor any others could make sense of."[5]

At first, the Reverend Parris and his wife, Elizabeth, thought the girls had an unknown illness. They called in the local doctor and asked his advice. The doctor examined the girls and prescribed an assortment of treatments. Nothing helped. At last, the doctor admitted that he could do no more. He told the Reverend Parris that the afflicted girls were clearly "under an evil hand."[6] Somehow, someone had bewitched them. Evil powers were being used against them.

As the weeks passed, Betty and Abigail grew steadily worse. Sometimes they trembled as if frightened. Their

Colonial Medicine

Doctors in colonial Massachusetts knew little about the causes of and cures for many diseases. Their treatments were sometimes worse than the illness they were trying to cure. One common treatment was bloodletting. Blood-sucking leeches were placed on the patient's body to draw out "impure" blood, which was thought to be causing the sickness.

Most medicines consisted of wine or ale mixed with a variety of herbs. Some remedies were more extreme. Drawing upon folk beliefs, these prescriptions today sound more like magic potions than medicines. The notebook of one Salem Town doctor contains a treatment for a condition he called "distractions" in women: "Take milk of [a woman who has given birth to] a male child, and also take a he-cat and cut off one of his ears or a piece of it, and let it bleed into the milk; and let the sick woman drink of it. Do this three times."[7]

bodies twisted uncontrollably. They cried out in pain, and screamed that someone was pinching them or pricking them with pins. By this time, witchcraft seemed the only explanation. The Reverend Parris spent hours each day praying for help, but the girls grew no better. By the end of January, all of Salem Village knew about the girls' afflictions. Neighbors stopped by to see for themselves the strange goings-on at the parsonage. The thought of witchcraft frightened them, but it excited them too. It gave people something to talk about on those long, cold winter evenings.

Late in February, the Reverend Parris traveled the seven miles to Salem Town. While he was away, Mary Sibley, a neighbor, attempted to free the girls from their supposed tormentor. Turning to an old folk remedy against witchcraft, she directed Tituba and John Indian to bake a "witch cake." The cake was made of rye flour mixed with the girls' urine. After the cake was baked, John and Tituba fed it to the family dog.

Some historians believe that the witch cake was a form of magic designed to hurt the witch. Others claim that the witch cake was supposed to help the girls recognize their tormentor. Whatever the cake's purpose, the Reverend Parris was outraged when he learned what had happened. Like fortune-telling, he saw the baking of a witch cake as the devil's work. He called Mary Sibley into his study and scolded her until she begged forgiveness. From the pulpit, he described what she had done and called on the congregation to vote on whether she should be forgiven. The congregation voted to forgive Mary Sibley with a unanimous show of hands.[8]

The terrifying signs of witchcraft in Salem Village were spreading. On the same day that John and Tituba baked the witch cake, two more girls reported demonic encounters. Seventeen-year-old Elizabeth Hubbard claimed that a wolf had chased her through the woods. She was certain that the wolf was actually a village woman named Sarah Good, traveling in the beast's form.

Elizabeth also claimed that another woman of the village, Sarah Osborne, pinched and pricked her mercilessly. Twelve-year-old Ann Putnam, Jr., announced that Sarah Good had come to her in a dream and tried to make her sign a mysterious book. She was sure it was the devil's book. Sarah Good wanted her to become the devil's servant.

Again and again, the Reverend Parris asked the girls who was pinching and pricking them. If they could name their tormentor, the person could be punished. Parris suggested names to the girls. He may have suggested people in the village who did not attend church regularly, or who seemed lazy or quarrelsome. Such an unsavory character, maybe even someone that had formed a pact with the devil, might be causing the girls' misery.

At last, Betty and Abigail told the Reverend Parris that they had glimpsed the shadowy form of their tormentor. They blamed their own servant, Tituba.

The men and women of Salem Village took these reports very seriously. They believed that the devil was constantly at work, trying to win souls away from God. Through trickery, the devil convinced ordinary women and men to help him. Female helpers, or disciples, were called witches. Males were known as wizards. When the girls twisted and screamed, most villagers believed that witchcraft caused the attacks. The devil had found

To the highly religious people of Salem, witches were definitely real.

disciples in Salem Village. The whole community was in danger.

On Monday, February 29, Ann Putnam's father and two other men made the long trip to Salem Town. They visited two magistrates, or judges—John Hathorne and Jonathan Corwin. The villagers charged Tituba, Sarah Good, and Sarah Osborne with "suspicion of witchcraft." According to the charges, there had been "much mischief done [to] Elizabeth Parris, Abigail Williams, Ann Putnam and Elizabeth Hubbard."[9] Judges Hathorne and Corwin ordered the arrest of the three women, who would be held for questioning.

These first three charges of witchcraft began one of the most tragic episodes in the history of colonial America. For nearly seven months, panic and fear swept eastern Massachusetts. Why did Salem Village become the scene of the most destructive witch-hunt in North American history? The answer is rooted in the history of witchcraft beliefs and witch-hunts in Europe and in the history of Salem Village itself.

Chapter 2

"Thou shalt not suffer [allow] a witch to live."
> —For hundreds of years, these words from the Bible (Exodus 22:18) were used to justify the hunting and killing of supposed witches in Europe and the New World.

In the long era of prehistory (until about 5000 B.C.) people lived in a world filled with mysteries. For unknown reasons, lightning slashed the skies and raging thunderclaps echoed among the mountains. Sometimes the sun was a gentle, life-giving force, and at other times it parched the crops and withered the leaves on the trees. No one understood what caused storms or droughts. No one knew why game was sometimes plentiful, and at other times so scarce that people went hungry.

Ancient peoples tried to make sense of the natural world that had such power in their lives. They believed that spirits lived in the sun and wind, the rocks and streams. Every living thing had a spirit of its own—fish, deer, wolves, owls, snakes, plants, and trees. Some spirits were kindly, and others were dangerous. Some were cruel to humans when they were angry, and generous when they were pleased.

In nearly every ancient society, certain people were thought to have special abilities to communicate with the spirit world. These persons knew how to ask the spirits for favors and to calm them when they were angry. In some cultures, such persons were called shamans or magicians. In others they were regarded as priests or priestesses. They had great power in the community. Often they were both respected and feared.

Ordinary members of the community might also find ways to gain special powers. A variety of rituals evolved, through which people enlisted the help of the spirits to reach their goals. Certain words, spoken under the full moon beside a sacred lake, for example, might heal the sick. Other words, uttered with the proper gestures, were thought to harm one's enemies. "Good magic" was connected with some objects, and "bad magic" with others.

Fighting Back Against the Devil

As the centuries passed, three major monotheistic religions arose in the Middle East. Followers of a monotheistic religion worship one supreme deity or god. Judaism emerged about five thousand years ago. Christianity was founded about two thousand years ago, and Islam developed around A.D. 600. One thing that the followers of Judaism, Christianity, and Islam had in common was that they all believed in a single god, an all-powerful deity who works for good in the world. However, traces of the old beliefs lingered on. Despite the establishment of new faiths, some people still believed in and practiced ancient forms of magic. In some communities, new and old religions existed side by side.

Christians saw God as the ultimate source of goodness. They found the source of the world's evil in Satan, or the devil. According to Christian beliefs, God and Satan were engaged in a constant struggle for the souls of human beings. The devil tempted humans to forget God's teachings and to break his commandments. Those who obeyed God and turned the devil aside would be rewarded in Heaven. Those who gave in to the devil's temptations would suffer eternal punishment in Hell.

During the period known as the Middle Ages (from A.D. 500 to 1500) the Christian Church became a powerful religious and political institution in western Europe. Few people could read and write. Since they were literate, Christian monks and priests were seen as knowledgeable and wise. For the common people, life was hard and often brief. A better day in Heaven was the only hope.

From 1347 to 1351, a terrible epidemic swept across Europe. Known as the Black Death, or the Great Plague, the disease killed as much as one-third of the European population within four years.[1] Farmers died before they could harvest their crops. Rich landowners died, leaving no one in charge of their properties. The monks and priests could do nothing to halt the disaster. The plague killed them, too.

The Black Death

Today, most scientists and historians believe that the Black Death was a disease known as bubonic plague. Fleas that live on the bodies of rats and other rodents carry bubonic plague. It is passed to humans through the bites of these fleas.

As if the plague were not bad enough, Europe was also wracked by a conflict known today as the Hundred Years War. The Hundred Years War was actually a series of conflicts that began in 1337 and did not end until 1453. The combination of plague and warfare ripped apart the fabric of European society. Landless laborers, known as peasants or serfs, struggled to seize property from the lords. New Christian groups, or sects, sprang up, challenging the power of what became the Roman Catholic Church.

The Catholic Church fought to maintain its power. Church officials violently suppressed the new sects. Members of these groups were called heretics. A heretic is someone who turns against established rules or beliefs. The Church also attacked other supposed enemies, including Muslim (Islamic) North Africans, or Moors, and Jews. Anyone who used herbs and spells to cure sickness or even anyone who behaved strangely could be suspected of defying the Church's authority. Under Church law, thousands of "enemies of God" were tried and put to death.

The Church claimed that anyone who did not follow its teachings was in league with the devil. It accused heretics, healers, and persons with signs of mental illness of practicing witchcraft. The Church fanned the fear of witches throughout Europe. By the late fifteenth century, a bloody witch-hunt known as the Great Inquisition had begun.

The Hammer of Witches

In 1484, Pope Innocent VIII issued a statement, or Papal bull, to all of the archbishops in Europe. The bull warned that dangerous numbers of Christians had "abandoned themselves to the Devil."[2] It gave Church officials full authority to find and put to death all those who had chosen to follow Satan's path. Two years later, a pair of German monks, Heinrich Kramer and Jakob Sprenger, published a massive book called the *Malleus Maleficarum*. The Latin title means *The Hammer of Witches*. The book was very popular. Between 1486 and 1669, it was reprinted thirty-four times.[3]

The *Malleus Maleficarum* described magical charms, spells, and rituals. It explained how witches could be recognized and captured. Finally, it instructed how witches should be tortured, tried, and executed. According to the book:

> Witchcraft is high treason against God's Majesty
> . . . and so [witches] are to be put to the torture
> in order to make them confess. Any person,
> whatever his rank or position, upon such an
> accusation may be put to the torture, and he

MALLEVS

MALEFICARVM,

MALEFICAS ET EARVM

hæresim frameâ conterens,

EX VARIIS AVCTORIBVS COMPILATVS,

& in quatuor Tomos iustè distributus,

QVORVM DVO PRIORES VANAS DÆMONVM versutias, præstigiosas eorum delusiones, superstitiosas Strigimagarum cæremonias, horrendos etiam cum illis congressus; exactam denique tam pestiferæ sectæ disquisitionem, & punitionem complectuntur. Tertius praxim Exorcistarum ad Dæmonum, & Strigimagarum maleficia de Christi fidelibus pellenda; Quartus verò Artem Doctrinalem, Benedictionalem, & Exorcismalem continent.

TOMVS PRIMVS.

Indices Auctorum, capitum, rerùmque non desunt.

Editio nouissima, infinitis penè mendis expurgata ; cuique accessit Fuga Dæmonum & Complementum artis exorcisticæ.

Vir siue mulier, in quibus Pythonicus, vel diuinationis fuerit spiritus, morte moriatur Leuitici cap. 10.

LVGDVNI,

Sumptibus CLAVDII BOVRGEAT, sub signo Mercurij Galli.

M. DC. LXIX.

CVM PRIVILEGIO REGIS.

This is the title page of a French edition of *Malleus Maleficarum*, a book on witchcraft and demonology, published in Lyons in 1669

who is found guilty, even if he confesses his
crime, let him be [tortured on the rack], let him
suffer all other tortures prescribed by law in
order that he may be punished in proportion to
his offenses.[4]

Kramer and Sprenger wrote from vast experience.
Before their book was published, they had executed some
fifty accused witches, mostly by sentencing them to burn
at the stake. Their writing was accepted as scholarship at
the time. "It is a most certain . . . opinion that there are
sorcerers and witches who by the help of the Devil, on
account of a compact which they have entered into with
him are able . . . to produce real and actual evils and
harm," they declared.[5] In horrifying detail, they depicted
the witches' bloody rituals: "Certain witches, against the
instinct of human nature . . . are in the habit of devour-
ing and eating infant children. . . . A certain man missed
his child from its cradle, and finding a congress of women
in the night-time, swore that he saw them kill his child and
drink its blood and devour it."[6] According to the book, a
witch could leave his or her body. Witches could fly great
distances at night and appear in the homes of neighbors
or strangers. Through evil magic, a witch could destroy
crops, burn houses, and sicken people and livestock.

In 1517, a German cleric named Martin Luther
nailed some sheets of paper to the door of a church in

Wittenberg. Luther's paper listed ninety-five criticisms of the Catholic Church. Luther's act of defiance launched a revolutionary movement called the Protestant Reformation. The new Protestant sects challenged many longstanding tenets of Roman Catholicism. However, they fully embraced the Church's beliefs about witchcraft. Luther himself believed that the Devil visited human beings to tempt and torment them, or simply to spread mischief.

In his writings, Luther described his own face-to-face meetings with Satan, whom he calls "the Old Gentleman." Luther said that one such encounter took place while he was imprisoned by Catholic bishops in a German castle. "Among other things," he wrote:

> [T]hey brought me hazel-nuts, which I put into
> a box, and sometimes I used to crack and eat of
> them. In the night-times, my gentleman, the
> Devil, came and got the nuts out of the box,
> and cracked them against one of the bedposts,
> making a very great noise and rumbling about
> my bed; but I regarded him nothing at all: when
> afterwards I began to slumber, then he kept such
> a racket and rumbling upon the chamber stairs,
> as if many empty barrels and hogsheads had
> been tumbled down.[7]

The Reformation triggered decades of turmoil in Europe. Throughout the upheaval, the Inquisition went on unabated. The Roman Catholic Church tried and executed witches under Church law. Wherever Protestantism took hold, officials of the new churches used civil, or state, law to convict witches and put them to death. Protestants and Roman Catholics alike believed that the Bible supported their crusade. They referred often to a verse from the Book of Exodus, which says, "Thou shalt not suffer [allow] a witch to live."

As Kramer and Sprenger recommended, officials often tortured suspected witches until they confessed. Questioners forced some suspects to sit for hours with their hands twisted behind their backs. Suspects could be kept awake for days on end, hounded with questions. Tortures bent suspects backward and tied them in agonizing positions. This torture was called "tying head to heels."

According to Sprenger and Kramer, most witches had one or more "familiars." A familiar was a demon that helped the witch carry out evil projects. It generally took the form of an animal, such as a cat, bird, or snake. The witch fed his or her familiar by letting it suck blood from the witch's body. For this reason, suspected witches were often examined for the presence of an abnormal bump on any part of the body, from which, it was thought, the familiar could suck blood.

Witches were thought to own or associate with strange animals and evil creatures called "familiars." Above, witches stand with a familiar (right).

Sometimes the questioners tested the suspect to determine guilt or innocence. The suspect might be forced to dip a hand into scalding water, or to hold a red-hot poker. It was thought that a witch's skin would not blister.

"Ducking" was the most famous test for witchcraft. The inquisitors tied the suspect's hands and feet and tossed the person into a deep pond. If the suspect floated, she or he was guilty, because the water rejected the unholy body. The suspect who sank was proved innocent—and, it was hoped, rescued before drowning. One expert on witchcraft explained, "The witch, having made a compact with the Devil, hath renounced her baptism, hence the antipathy between her and water."[8]

Witchcraft experts believed that a witch could leave his or her body at night and travel freely. The witch might appear to others far away. Sometimes the witch could easily be recognized, but at other times would appear in the form of an animal. The witch might also appear to a bewitched person in a dream. The report of any such sighting was called spectral evidence. Spectral evidence was the most problematic proof of witchcraft. It was very hard to prove that a witch's spirit had actually been seen. It was nearly impossible, however, to prove that the witch's spirit had *not* appeared.

Once accused of witchcraft, a person was doomed. If the suspect confessed under torture, the confession was accepted as proof by the courts. If she or he insisted on innocence, the suspect could be accused of resisting the authorities. One woman in Scotland made this statement to a crowd of onlookers before she went to the gallows:

> I declare I am as free of witchcraft as any child
> . . . but, being [denounced] by a malicious

woman, and put in prison under the name of a witch, disowned by my husband and friends, and seeing no ground of hope of my coming out of prison, or ever coming in credit again, . . . I made up that confession on purpose to destroy my own life, being weary of it, and choosing rather to die than live.[9]

After the publication of *Malleus Maleficarum*, many other scholars and church leaders wrote about witchcraft.

In Europe, people found guilty of witchcraft were sometimes burned at the stake.

Their works supported and strengthened the public's deeply held beliefs. A few courageous physicians raised their voices in protest. They argued that illness, rather than witchcraft, caused convulsions and other symptoms. Their arguments were largely ignored. Established religion carried far more weight than the theories of science.

Some scholars claim that about thirty thousand people were killed for witchcraft in Europe between 1400 and 1600. Others believe the numbers were far higher,

This colored engraving shows a public hanging of accused witches in Scotland in 1678.

perhaps reaching the millions. After careful study of surviving records, one historian concluded that about two hundred thousand people were accused of witchcraft, and one hundred thousand were put to death.[10] When immigrants from Europe began to settle in North America in the 1600s, they carried their deep fear of witches across the Atlantic.

Witches in the Wilderness

The first English settlers in New England found a land of enormous bounty. The woods teemed with game, and vast schools of fish swam in the coastal waters. Yet the newcomers also met hardship and danger. Not even a roaring fire could keep the house warm in the dead of winter. In his diary, the Boston preacher Cotton Mather said that the ink froze as he wrote. The kitchen was so cold, he claimed, that ice formed on the ends of the logs in the fireplace.[11]

Worse still was the constant fear of American Indian raids. Because the Indians were not Christians, most settlers saw them as the devil's tools. Strife between the settlers and the American Indians served to strengthen this opinion. Sometimes the Indians attacked isolated farms or villages. A bloody conflict between settlers and Indians, known as King Philip's War, broke out in 1675. The war went on for two years. Occasional fighting persisted into the 1690s.

King Philip's War

The story of Thanksgiving is well-known throughout the United States. A Wampanoag Indian chief named Massasoit helped the people of the struggling Plymouth Colony to survive their first year. Together the colonists and their Wampanoag rescuers shared a feast of celebration.

Far less well-known is the story of King Philip's War, which erupted a little more than fifty years later. By 1675, the English colonists had crowded the Wampanoag off most of their land. The way of life of the Wampanoag was steadily being destroyed. Metacom, the son of Massasoit, decided to take a stand. Because of his boldness, the English nicknamed him King Philip. Metacom promised, "I am determined not to live until I have no country."[12]

Metacom united several American Indian groups to resist the English. Indian bands attacked numerous towns along the Connecticut River in western Massachusetts. Both Indians and colonists suffered heavy losses. The war finally ended when colonists killed Metacom in August 1676.

Most of the early English settlers in Massachusetts belonged to a religious group called the Puritans. The Puritans did not agree with the established Church of England. They sought to purify the church—that is, to return it to the basic teachings of the Bible. The Puritans believed that life should be dedicated to the worship of God. They felt that the devil was always looking for chances to lead people astray. Dancing, games, fancy clothes, and lively music were invitations to Satan. So were quarrels, spitefulness, and jealousy. Preachers urged their followers to speak kindly to one another and to put petty disputes aside. Everyone was expected to work together and contribute to the community as a whole.

Everyone in the community was expected to attend church services. Yet only a handful of people were considered full-fledged church members, sometimes referred to as the "visible saints." To become a church member, a man or woman had to be sober, law-abiding, hardworking, and, preferably, well-to-do. As a final step, the person had to present a "conversion narrative" to the church's pastor. The conversion narrative was an account of the prospective member's spiritual life. It was intended to show that the person had been granted God's grace. Church members held most of the political power in the community.[13]

In a world full of illness, accidents, American Indian attacks, and other perils, the Puritans prayed for guidance and protection. When tragedy struck, they looked for explanations. Perhaps a baby died because God was angry with the parents for failing to go to church. Perhaps a witch or wizard had sickened the baby. If illness or bad luck followed a dispute with a neighbor, witchcraft was a strong possibility. Perhaps the neighbor had gained supernatural powers by making a pact with Satan. When angry, the neighbor might cast a spell to cause harm.

In 1647, a deadly epidemic broke out near Windsor, Connecticut. People accused Alice Young of using witchcraft to cause the epidemic. Young was tried, convicted, and hanged for her crime. She is thought to be the first person executed for witchcraft in the English colonies.

Settlers worship at a church in Plymouth, Massachusetts.

In the decades that followed, authorities held many more witchcraft trials in Connecticut and Massachusetts. According to court records, at least ninety-three women and men were tried for witchcraft in these two colonies before the Salem outbreak. Sixteen of these suspects were convicted and hanged.[14]

As the records show, many accused witches were acquitted. Even those found guilty were not always put to death. Elizabeth Morse of Newbury, Massachusetts, was convicted of witchcraft but managed to avoid the gallows. In 1679, her grandson, John Stiles, began to have strange episodes referred to as "fits." A witness reported that sometimes he was "flung about in such a manner as they feared that his brains would have been beaten out." He screamed that someone or something was pricking him, and tried to throw himself into the fire. Now and then he barked like a dog. He even tried to eat sticks, ashes, and yarn.[15] Elizabeth Morse was convicted of bewitching her grandson and sentenced to die. However, her husband pleaded on her behalf, and the colonial legislature was unwilling to carry out the sentence. Lawmakers delayed the hanging and eventually Elizabeth Morse was released from jail.

Another accused witch was a Salem Town woman named Bridget Bishop. In 1680, a farmer named Samuel Gray accused her of entering his room at night in spectral form and sitting on his chest. Bridget Bishop was found not guilty. Robert Calef, who wrote an account of the Salem witchcraft trials in 1700, states that "upon his deathbed [Gray] testified his sorrow and repentance for such accusations, as being wholly groundless."[16] Nevertheless, Bishop never quite lived down the accusation.

One famous witchcraft trial took place in Boston in 1688. A thirteen-year-old girl, Martha Goodwin, went to the local laundress to collect the family's washing. When she looked at the bundle of clean clothes, she noticed that some items were missing. Martha accused the laundress of stealing. The laundress was furious. Her mother, an Irish woman known as the Widow Glover, joined the argument. Glover cursed at Martha and told her she would suffer for making false accusations.

A few days later Martha Goodwin had strange fits. Three of her younger brothers and sisters were soon afflicted as well. The Reverend Cotton Mather observed the children, especially Martha, and wrote at length about everything he saw. According to Mather, the Goodwin children "would fly like geese, and be carried with an incredible swiftness, having but just their toes now and then upon the ground, sometimes not once in twenty feet, and their arms waved like the wings of a bird."[17] Glover was convicted of bewitching the children. She confessed to the crime and was hanged.

The story of the Goodwin children was known throughout New England. By the winter of 1692, Betty Parris and Abigail Williams may have heard the strange and frightening tale. The case of the Widow Glover helped set the stage for the witchcraft trials in Salem. Yet many other factors also prepared the way for the tragedy that began to unfold in the Reverend Parris's kitchen.

In 1682, a Salem Village resident named Jeremiah Watts wrote a letter to the village minister, George Burroughs. In his letter, Watts declared that the village seethed with bickering and discontent. "Brother is against brother and neighbors [are] against neighbors," he wrote, "all quarreling and smiting one another."[1] The witchcraft crisis of 1692 sprang up as this atmosphere of unrest clouded the New England village.

The Lonely Village

In 1620, the Pilgrims founded Plymouth Colony on the coast of present-day Massachusetts. Eight years later, in 1628, a merchant named Roger Conant established a small settlement on the coast farther north. He named it Salem. Perched on a neck of land, Salem overlooked a fine harbor. Conant and his followers hoped it would become a thriving center of trade.

At first Salem prospered. Merchant ships brought molasses from the West Indies and textiles from England. They carried away timber from the New England forests and dried cod from the fisheries along the coast. The town expanded quickly. In 1639, the General Court (the governing body in Boston) allowed Salem to spread westward to the Ipswich River. Salem residents were given land that they could clear for farming. The outlying settlement, which remained part of Salem Town, was called Salem Farms.

At first, Salem Farms was a scattered collection of houses surrounded by woods and fields. It had no church, no courthouse, and no village square where people could gather. For business and worship the Salem Farmers had to make the long journey back to Salem Town. They paid taxes to Salem Town and attended church services there on Sundays. Town officials, called selectmen, set the prices that Salem Farmers could charge for grain in the Salem Town market. Men from Salem Farms were required to serve on the Salem Town Watch, an unpaid police force.

As the years passed, many of the people in Salem Farms grew discontent. In 1667, thirty Salem Farms residents asked the General Court to be relieved of their duty on the Salem Town Watch. "Some of us live ten miles, some eight or nine; the nearest are at least five miles from Salem meeting-house," the petition stated, "so that some of us must travel armed eleven miles to watch—which is more than a soldier's march that is under pay."[2] They pointed out that the scattered houses of Salem Farms were very vulnerable to American Indian raids, and asked "whether Salem Town hath not more cause to send us help to watch among ourselves than we have to go to them?"[3] The General Court ruled that men who lived more than four miles from the Salem Town meetinghouse need not serve on the Town Watch. However, the town did not heed the court's ruling. In 1669, two men from Salem Farms were fined for refusing to serve and were forced to make a public apology.

For some of the Salem Farms families, the trip to attend church each Sunday was nearly impossible. Many of the people of Salem Farms longed for a meetinghouse of their own. They wanted their own minister, who could preach to them on Sundays and counsel them in times of need. Again and again, the Salem Farmers asked Salem Town to let them build a meetinghouse. Every time their request was ignored. The matter came to a head in 1669, when taxes were raised to pay for a new Salem Town meetinghouse. A group from Salem Farms refused to pay the tax "unless you likewise of the Town will share with us when we shall build [a meetinghouse] for ourselves."[4] Two Salem Farmers raised the issue at a meeting in Salem Town. At first they were ignored. When they finally managed to speak, they were told that their request was out of order.[5]

After three more years of pleas and refusals from Salem Farms, the Salem Town selectmen finally agreed to let Salem Farms build a meetinghouse. The meetinghouse served as a spiritual center for the scattered farming community. By the time Salem Town authorized the

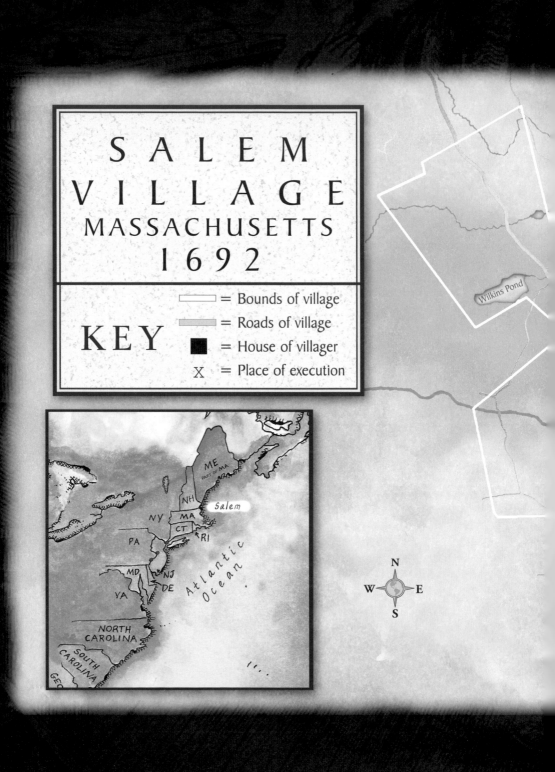

SALEM VILLAGE
MASSACHUSETTS
1692

KEY

☐ = Bounds of village
▬ = Roads of village
■ = House of villager
X = Place of execution

Wilkins Pond

ME
PART OF MA

NH

Salem

NY   MA
CT   RI

PA

MD
VA   NJ
DE   *Atlantic Ocean*

NORTH
CAROLINA

SOUTH
CAROLINA

GEO

N
W   E
S

A Voice for Every Man

In colonial days, New England towns held regular meetings. At a town meeting, any man in the community was free to speak. (Women did not participate directly.) Discussions at town meetings helped resolve a range of issues related to the town's government. Anyone could raise his concerns or make suggestions. The practice of holding town meetings survives in many parts of New England to this day. However, women now participate, too.

meetinghouse late in 1672, the name Salem Farms had changed to Salem Village.

The new meetinghouse spared the villagers the long trip into Salem Town on Sundays. However, it created a fresh set of problems. The village had to choose a minister. Who should make this important choice? Since the minister would serve the whole village, perhaps all of the village's voting men should make the selection. On the other hand, the village's church members felt that they alone should have the final say. After all, church members were the most powerful and respected people in the community.

The first Salem Village minister, James Bayley, was chosen by a general vote of all the Village men. From the beginning, the church members resented the choice and the way it had been made. Over the next seven years, some factions in the village supported Bayley while others pushed to dismiss him. At last, Bayley resigned and moved to Connecticut, weary of what he called "uncomfortable divisions and contentions."[6]

The next two ministers in Salem Village fared no

better. George Burroughs, a refugee from the American Indian wars in Maine, was appointed in 1680. He returned to Maine after serving the village for only three years. When he left, the village still owed him most of his salary. Burroughs was followed by Deodat Lawson, who held on until 1688. He too left after years of wrangling.

None of the first three Salem Village ministers had been ordained. To be ordained, a minister needed the approval of a body of ministers from several established churches. Only an ordained minister could baptize babies and perform the Christian ceremony known as Communion. In the Communion ritual, church members eat bread and drink wine from a shared cup. The bread

This replica of the Salem Village meetinghouse was built on the land where Rebecca Nurse once lived.

and wine represent the body and blood of Jesus Christ. For the Puritans, taking Communion was an extremely important part of worship.

Samuel Parris was the fourth minister to arrive in Salem Village. He and his family settled into the parsonage in 1689. Like Bayley, Burroughs, and Lawson, Parris was chosen by the village's voters rather than by its church members. The voters also decided that the new minister should be ordained. Parris's ordination made the Salem Village meetinghouse a true church. Within a year, fifty-three men and women of the village—about one-fourth of its adult population—had become village church members. Longstanding members of the church in Salem Town felt uneasy about the village church and its flock of new members. They feared that the new meetinghouse would take members away from the Salem Town church and undermine its power.

Now that the village had a church of its own, a group of Salem Village residents pushed for complete independence from Salem Town. Nothing came of the request. Town and village remained tethered to one another, but the rift between them steadily widened. So, too, did the differences between groups of families within the village itself.

Neighbor Against Neighbor

In 1682, a man named Jeremiah Watts penned an impassioned description of Salem Village. He claimed that the village could never become an independent town due to its endless strife. Arguments and feuds are part of life for people nearly everywhere. However, the uncertain status of Salem Village added to its troubles. The village had no courthouse or governing body, so disputes had to be settled in Salem Town. Furthermore, some villagers felt greater loyalty to Salem Town than did others. The situation was a recipe for grievances and bitterness.

The Putnams and the Porters were two of the most influential families in Salem Village. The Porters owned land on the eastern edge of the village, the side closest to Salem Town. Although they did some farming, they were mainly involved in trade. John Porter and his sons ran sawmills in Salem Village. Several Porter women married into merchant families of Salem Town. The Porters served as selectmen in the Salem Town government and held positions in the Salem Town church.

The Putnams, on the other hand, were farmers who owned land on the northwestern side of Salem Village. As fathers passed land on to their sons over the years, the Putnam holdings were divided into smaller and smaller tracts. Most of the Putnams attended the Salem Village church, and a number of them were church members.

Overall, the Porters tended to look toward Salem Town and the world beyond it. The Putnams remained deeply connected to the village and uninvolved with the world outside.

Considering their differences, it is not surprising that tension arose between the Porter and Putnam families. Court records show that Thomas Putnam brought a lawsuit against John Porter in 1672. Putnam complained that a dam flooded the access road to his farm at one of Porter's sawmills. The flooding was so severe that the road was impassable for months at a time. "To be this long kept prisoner," Putnam told the court, "will be the way to ruin me and mine forever."[7]

The Putnams had problems with other Salem Village families as well. For years they were tangled in a boundary dispute with a neighbor, Francis Nurse. They sued George Burroughs to repay his debt after he borrowed money to pay for his wife's funeral. (Burroughs had to borrow money because the village had failed to pay him most of his salary.)

Though they had enemies in both Salem Town and Salem Village, the Putnams also had strong allies. They were especially loyal to the minister of Salem Village, Samuel Parris. When Parris was offered the position in the village, he spent months negotiating his salary and other benefits. A village committee, led by several Putnams and their supporters, agreed to give the parsonage and two acres of land to the Parris family. The decision swept aside an ordinance passed by the committee in 1681, by which the parsonage belonged to the village forever. The court record granting the parsonage to the Parris family simply declares that the earlier law "is hereby made void and of no effect."[8]

Many villagers felt that Samuel Parris had no right to own the parsonage; they thought he should only be allowed to live there while he was minister. The controversy started his ministry on a jarring note. It helped to establish two factions that were fiercely opposed to one another. One faction supported Samuel Parris, and the other was against him. Like the village ministers before him, the Reverend Parris saw trouble ahead.

Murmurs From the Wider World

Massachusetts was an English colony. However, for decades in the late seventeenth century, it enjoyed a generous share of self-government. England allowed Massachusetts to choose its own leaders, levy its own taxes, and set its own prices on trade goods. The colonists were also free to buy and sell land as they saw fit.

In July 1685, a ship sailed into Boston Harbor bearing terrible news. The year before, King Charles II had revoked the royal charter that allowed these rights.

A newly crowned king, James II, had appointed a royal governor—Sir Edmund Andros. He would have authority over a vast territory called the Dominion of New England. Andros' territory sprawled from Maine to parts of present-day New Jersey.

Andros quickly lived up to the worst fears of the Massachusetts colonists. Under his rule, town meetings could be held only once a year. Only local decisions were within the colonists' control. The English Crown claimed ownership of all of their land. The crown would lease its land to the colonists for a fee. Families who had worked their own farms for generations suddenly found that they were landless tenants.

Appalled by these changes, the people of Massachusetts sent one of their most trusted leaders to plead for them in London. Their ambassador was Increase Mather, a Boston minister and scholar. (His son, Cotton Mather, had followed him into the ministry.) In London, Increase Mather began negotiating for a return to the old charter. Meanwhile, the people in the Dominion of New England grew impatient. In the fall of 1689, rebels in Boston overcame the redcoated soldiers Andros had brought from England. The rebels jailed Andros. The governor was helpless, leaving Massachusetts with no government at all.

As New England waited for word from London, fighting with the American Indians flared again. In 1691,

Algonquin war parties attacked settlements in Maine and New Hampshire. Raiders struck isolated farms along the Merrimac River in Massachusetts. When the nearby town of Rowley was attacked, people in Salem Village were frightened. They wondered if they would be next.

In this troubled time, rumors of witchcraft bubbled to the surface. In September 1691, Mary Randall was arrested for witchcraft and questioned in Springfield, Massachusetts. She was released on bail. A month later, Martha Sparks of Chelmsford, Massachusetts, was also charged with witchcraft. She was sent to jail in Boston to await trial. With the colony in chaos, no one had the authority to try the case.[9] Far away in England, William of Orange from the Netherlands succeeded King James. Increase Mather had to begin his negotiations again with a brand-new ruler. King William made it clear that he would never restore the old charter to Massachusetts. Mather was forced to accept a compromise.

The colonists would once again have the right to pass their own laws and levy their own taxes. Titles to their land would be returned to them. However, the king would appoint the governor of the colony. And, to Mather's dismay, non-church members would now be allowed to hold office. The new charter was a big step toward offering religious freedom to Protestants who were not Puritans. "It is not so bad," Mather wrote about the new charter. "Take it with all its faults and it is not so

Even before the Salem Village witchcraft trials of 1692, people were sometimes accused of witchcraft in Massachusetts.

bad but when I left New England the inhabitants . . . would gladly have parted with many a thousand pounds to have obtained one so good."[10]

The king favored the idea of appointing Sir Edmund Andros governor once more. Increase Mather convinced him that Andros's reappointment would trigger an angry uprising. Mather recommended Sir William Phips, who was already well-known to the colonists. The king appointed Phips to serve as the new governor of Massachusetts.

Pirate Phips

The story of Sir William Phips is filled with high adventure. Phips was one of twenty-six children, twenty-one of them boys. He grew up on a struggling farm in the Maine wilderness. (Maine was part of the Massachusetts colony at that time.) Cotton Mather later described Phips's early home as "a despicable plantation on the river of the Kennebec."[11] Phips was determined to rise in the world. When he was twenty-one, he learned to read and write and apprenticed himself to a ship's carpenter. When he had mastered the carpenter's trade, he moved to Boston to find work. There he married the daughter of a wealthy family. According to Mather, he promised her that someday she would live in "a fair brick house in the Green Lane of Boston."[12]

Through hard work and good luck, Phips became a ship's captain. On a voyage to the West Indies he discovered a sunken Spanish ship loaded with treasure. He and his crew raised six tons of gold, silver, pearls, and other jewels. The discovery of the Spanish treasure earned Phips the nickname Pirate Phips. It also earned him the rank of Knight of the Order of the Golden Fleece from King James II. After turning over most of the treasure to the crown, he became Sir William Phips.

Sir William Phips and Increase Mather sailed for Boston in the spring of 1692. Phips was deeply committed to the people of New England. "I knew that if God had a people . . . it was here," he stated, "and I resolved to rise and fall with them."[13] Yet, as his ship drew near the New England coast, Phips had no hint of the challenge that awaited him. He could not have guessed that his first duty as governor would be to handle a witchcraft outbreak in Salem Village.

Chapter 4

On the chilly morning of March 1, 1692, John Hathorne and Jonathan Corwin rode out to Salem Village from Salem Town. The two magistrates found the village in an uproar. The villagers knew that the magistrates were coming to question the accused witches. They wanted to watch every scene of the unfolding drama. They did not want to miss a word.

"Why Do You Hurt These Children?"

Noisy spectators crowded the meetinghouse. They watched as Sarah Good, the first of the three suspects, was led to the front of the room. Goody Good, as she was called in the village, had been born into a well-to-do family, but she had fallen on hard times. Her husband seldom worked, and the family was often homeless. Good had begged door-to-door for food for herself and her children. People said she muttered curses if they did not give her enough. Sometimes misfortunes befell her neighbors soon after she departed.

In American courts today, a suspect is presumed innocent until proven guilty. Judges Corwin and Hathorne did not work from this premise. John Hathorne's first question to Sarah Good assumed her guilt. "Sarah Good," he asked, "what evil spirit have you familiarity with?"

Terms of Address

In colonial New England the terms "Goodman" and "Goodwife" were generally used in referring to people of the working classes. A man named Thomas Brown was called Goodman Brown, and his wife Sarah would be Goodwife (often shortened to Goody) Brown. People of the wealthier classes were known as Mister or Mistress.

"None," Sarah Good replied.

Hathorne was not satisfied. "Have you made no contract with the devil?" he pursued. When Sarah Good said "No," the magistrate asked her, "Why do you hurt these children?"

Sarah Good held her ground. "I do not hurt them," she stated. "I scorn it."

Judge Hathorne tried a different strategy. "What creature do you employ then?" he wanted to know.

Sarah Good did not waver. "No creature," she told him, "but I am falsely accused."[1]

Judge Hathorne then questioned William Good, Sarah Good's husband. Rather than defending his wife, William spoke against her. He told the judges "that he was afraid that she either was a witch or would be one very quickly."[2] He had never seen her perform witchcraft, he admitted, but there was something devilish in her behavior toward him. Furthermore, he pointed out, she had a small wart near her right shoulder that might very well be the place where a familiar sucked her blood.

For final proof Judge Hathorne turned to the four bewitched girls. He asked them if Sarah Good was one of the persons who tormented them. The girls cried out that she was. As if to prove their point they began to scream, choke, and writhe. Deodat Lawson, who witnessed similar fits on several occasions, wrote:

> Sometimes . . . they have had their tongues drawn out of their mouths to a fearful length, their heads turned very much over their shoulders; and while they have been so strained in their fits, and had their arms and legs, etc, wrested as if they were quite dislocated, the blood hath gushed plentifully out of their mouths . . . I saw several together thus violently strained and bleeding in their fits, to my very great astonishment that my fellow-mortals should be so grievously distressed by the invisible powers of darkness.[3]

Seeing the girls in agony and hearing their shrieks, the spectators and the judges reached a firm conclusion. Sarah Good was to blame. The judges ordered her back to jail and called in the next suspect, Sarah Osborne.

Like Sarah Good, Sarah Osborne was an outsider in Salem Village. She had shocked the villagers by marrying one of her servants. She seldom went to church, claiming that she was ill. A complicated legal case over the inheritance of a piece of land had put her at odds with the powerful Putnam family.[4]

Now Sarah Osborne, a frail old woman, stood before the judges. Again, Judge Hathorne asked the suspect questions. Again, the accused witch denied that she had ever hurt the girls. For a second time the girls were asked to look at the accused. Their fits broke out afresh, as noisy and violent as before. Sarah Osborne was taken to join Sarah Good in jail.

It was time to question the last of the suspected witches, the slave known as Tituba. At first she, too, denied practicing witchcraft. As Judge Hathorne persisted, however, she suddenly burst out with an astonishing story. She declared that the devil had appeared to her and

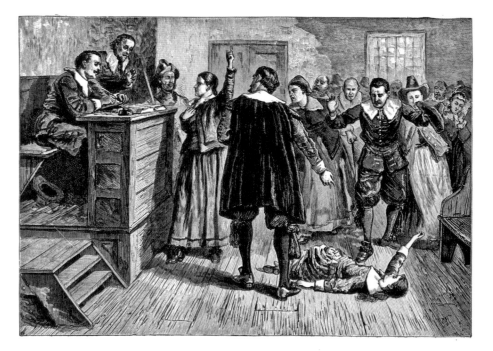

The afflicted girls threw fits during the initial hearing for Sarah Good.

Tituba said that the devil, dressed in black, appeared to her in the woods.

ordered her to serve him. He had sent his messengers to speak with her. They came to her in the forms of a pig, two cats, and a big black dog. The devil's messengers urged her to hurt the girls, threatening to harm her if she refused. At last she gave in, though she stated, "I am very sorry for it." Tituba also claimed that she had seen Sarah Good and Sarah Osborne torturing the girls. The spectral shapes of two other women and a man from Boston were also involved. Sarah Good, she claimed, had a little yellow bird as her familiar. Two familiars served Sarah Osborne, "a thing with a head like a woman with 2 leggs [sic] and wings," and a hairy little creature that walked upright like a man.[5]

The judges and the spectators listened in amazement. Even the girls fell silent, spellbound by Tituba's tale. Here at last was the evidence everyone had waited to hear. The devil walked among them. Tituba had seen him with her own eyes. Satan had ensnared three village women and tormented four innocent girls. Where would he strike next? Was anyone truly safe?

Naming the Specters

After the hearings, Sarah Good, Sarah Osborne, and Tituba were taken to jail in Boston to await trial. However, the torments of the girls in Salem Village continued. In fact, they grew more frequent and violent. Tituba said that other witches remained at large. The villagers wondered who they were. When would the girls reveal their names?

It did not take long for the girls to identify a new set of witches. Ann Putnam, Jr., reported that Dorcas Good, Sarah Good's four-year-old daughter, appeared to her and held out a book for her to sign. Ann said she knew it was the devil's book and refused to touch it. Enraged, Dorcas scratched, bit, pinched, and choked her.

Dorcas was not Ann's only tormentor. Ann announced that the spectral shape of a village woman named Martha Corey had also pinched her and pricked her. This was alarming news. Unlike the other accused witches, Martha Corey was a member of the village church. Two church members, Ezekiel Cheever and Edward Putnam, decided to have a talk with Corey.[6] Edward Putnam was Ann Putnam's uncle. His brother, Thomas Putnam, Jr., was Ann's father.

Before they headed to the Corey farm, Cheever and Putnam questioned Ann about Martha Corey's visits. They asked what clothes Corey had been wearing when Ann saw her. If they found her wearing the clothes Ann described, then Corey's guilt was assured. Ann, however, was of no help. As Cheever later wrote, she told them that the specter "came and blinded her but told her that her name was Corey and that she should see her no more before it was night because she should not tell us what clothes she had on."[7]

Perhaps rumors of the men's visit flew ahead of them to Martha Corey's house. When the men arrived, Corey seemed to be expecting them. She even guessed that they were investigating the story that she was a witch. To the men's amazement, she asked if they had come to see what clothes she was wearing. To them, it was as if she magically knew what they were thinking and planning. Martha Corey seemed calm. Her boldness and her mysterious knowledge convinced the men that she probably was a witch. Her church membership made no difference. The devil had slipped into the church itself!

Still another specter haunted Ann Putnam, Jr. It began tormenting her mother and the family servant, Mercy Lewis, as well. Abigail Williams also claimed to have seen it. Mercy Lewis and Ann Putnam, Sr., asked Ann, Jr., if she could identify this latest specter. After some thought Ann named another church member, Rebecca Nurse.

A feeble woman of seventy-one, Rebecca Nurse was beloved by her large family and highly respected in the village. However, her mother had once been suspected of witchcraft, though she was never taken to trial. Witchcraft was thought to be passed down in families from mother to daughter. Was it possible that Rebecca Nurse, so gentle and pious, might be a witch, too?

Four friends and supporters went to the Nurse farm to tell Rebecca Nurse of the accusations against her. Among them were Israel and Elizabeth Porter, longtime foes of the Putnam family. They described their visit in a detailed letter, which they presented, to the court. Rebecca Nurse was pleased to see them and had no idea why they had come. She even told them she had been praying for the afflicted girls. When her friends explained the reason for their visit, "she sat still awhile, being as it were amazed," her friends wrote. "And then she said,

The afflicted girls react as a judge questions Rebecca Nurse.

'Well, as to this thing, I am as innocent as the child unborn. But surely, what sin hath God found out in me unrepented of that He should lay such an affliction upon me in my old age.'"[8] Nurse quietly assumed that the accusation was God's punishment for some past sin she must have committed.

Dorcas Good, Martha Corey, and Rebecca Nurse were all arrested and questioned in the village

Locked Away

The accused witches were scattered among several Massachusetts jails. Some were held in Salem Town, some in Ipswich, and several in Boston. No matter where they were imprisoned, the conditions were horrifying. The floors were filthy. Jailers crammed three or more prisoners into each cell. The accused shared their quarters with lice, rats, and fleas. Because they were considered dangerous, the accused witches were chained to the walls. Each prisoner was required to pay a weekly fee. An additional fee was charged for renting the shackles![11]

meetinghouse. Whenever they looked at their accusers, the afflicted girls howled, twisted, choked, and screamed. They shouted that a band of witches were mustering in front of the meetinghouse, and Deodat Lawson noted that they asked Corey, "Did she not hear the drum beat?"[9] Swept up by the girls' distress, the spectators cried and screamed as well. "The whole assembly were struck with consternation," wrote Lawson, "and were afraid that those who sat next to them were under the influence of witchcraft."[10] The tumult in the meetinghouse was seen as evidence that the three newest suspects were guilty. They, too, were taken to jail to await trial.

Shortly before Martha Corey's hearing, the Reverend Deodat Lawson visited Samuel Parris's parsonage. There he witnessed the bizarre behavior of Abigail Williams. Lawson wrote that Abigail "was at first hurryed [sic] with Violence to and fro in the room, . . . sometimes makeing [sic] as if she would fly, stretching up her arms as high as she could, and crying, 'Whish, Whish, Whish!' several times."

She even rushed to the fireplace and began "to throw fire brands [burning sticks] about the house."[12] Such behavior by a young girl was unheard of. Lawson watched in fascinated horror.

In Puritan New England, girls and young women were expected to be quiet and reserved. Even girls as young as Abigail Williams and Ann Putnam, Jr., had chores at home that filled their days. Now, they shrieked and writhed and raced about and neglected their household duties. Instead of being punished for creating a disturbance, the girls were comforted and fussed over. Deodat Lawson and other leading men of the church asked them careful questions and wrote down everything they said. Surely the afflicted girls of Salem Village had never had such lavish attention in all their lives.

Not everyone in Salem believed that witches tormented the girls. One of the doubters was a farmer, John Proctor. He told a neighbor that the afflicted girls "should rather be had to the whipping post, [for] if they were let alone so we should all be devils and witches quickly." When his sixteen-year-old servant-girl, Mary Warren, was taken with fits, Proctor had no patience. He told his neighbor that "when she was first taken with fits he kept her close to the [spinning] Wheel & threatened to thresh her, & then she had no more fits."[13] When her fits disappeared, Mary asked the congregation to give a prayer of thanks. She was even heard to comment that "the afflicted persons did but dissemble [lie]."[14]

Listening to the Drumbeat

The Sunday after Martha Corey and Rebecca Nurse were arrested, Samuel Parris gave a sermon in Salem Village. In the sermon titled, "Christ Knows How Many Devils There Are in His Churches, and Who They Are," Parris warned that members of the church had become devils by working with Satan. "Oh it is a dreadful thing to be a devil," he declared, "and yet to sit down at the Lord's table."[15] The Reverend Parris had barely begun to preach when a woman rose from her pew. She was Sarah Cloyce, the younger sister of Rebecca Nurse. Refusing to listen to the sermon, she walked out of the church and slammed the door behind her. Surely she was thinking of her sister, a devoted church member, who suffered in a Boston jail. On April 4, Cloyce, like her sister, was arrested for witchcraft.

The afflicted girls had warned that a small army of witches was mustering in Salem Village. Now it seemed that more and more people in and around Salem Village heard the dreadful drumbeat. Seventeen-year-old Mary Walcott had fits. Two married women in their thirties, Bathshua Pope and Sarah Bibber, reported being pinched and tormented. Men, too, were among the afflicted. John Indian, the husband of the suspected witch Tituba, began

Martha Corey pleads for mercy during her trial.

to shriek and writhe. Farmer Benjamin Gould claimed that he woke one night to find the spectral forms of several witches hovering around his bed. Among them he recognized Martha Corey and her eighty-year-old husband, Giles. He also saw John and Elizabeth Proctor, and the sisters Rebecca Nurse and Sarah Cloyce. Soon Giles

Corey and the Proctors were arrested and locked in jail with the others.

Mary Warren had stated that the afflicted persons dissembled, meaning that they had lied. It was not long before John Indian and several of the afflicted girls accused Mary of hurting them. Mary Warren, who had been among the afflicted only days before, found herself being questioned by the magistrates. She declared her innocence, but the afflicted girls shrieked and broke into violent convulsions. Overcome, Mary fainted. "I will tell, I will tell," she muttered as she regained consciousness. Yet she could not explain what she wanted to reveal. She seemed to be choking, and she spoke no words.[16] She was sent to jail, where her own torments resumed in full force. An accused witch, she was also among the afflicted.

Like a landslide or avalanche, the witchcraft accusations gathered momentum. They reached beyond Salem Village into the neighboring communities. Bridget Bishop was arrested in Salem Town. Three women from Topsfield were arrested—Sarah Wildes and Abigail and Deliverance Hobbs, a mother and stepdaughter. In Andover, Martha Carrier was arrested for shaking and threatening eleven-year-old Phebe Chandler while in spectral form. Lydia Dustin of Reading, Susanna Martin of Amesbury, and Dorcas Hoar and Sarah Morrell of Beverly were all arrested. They were accused of tormenting Mary

Walcott, Mercy Lewis, Abigail Williams, Ann Putnam, Jr., Elizabeth Hubbard, and a newly afflicted girl named Susanna Sheldon.[17] In Stamford, Connecticut, more than two hundred miles south of Salem Village, a servant named Katherine Branch fell to the floor, writhing and moaning in pain. She accused two local women, Elizabeth Clawson and Mercy Disborough, of tormenting her. Both suspects were arrested and held for trial.

The most astonishing accusation of all came from Abigail Williams and Ann Putnam in late April. One day Ann suddenly cried out, "Oh, dreadful! dreadful! here is a minister come! What! Are ministers witches too?"[18] Abigail Williams described the torturing specter of a small dark man. Both girls declared that their latest tormentor was none other than former Salem Village minister George Burroughs.

By this time, Burroughs had a new congregation in Wells, Maine. He had never met the girls who accused him. Nevertheless, constables set out for Maine to make their arrest. Soon, George Burroughs, once the most important man in Salem Village, sat in the Salem Town jail.

In most cases, the afflicted swore that the accused hurt them and tried to make them sign the devil's book. During the hearings, they screamed and twisted whenever the accused spoke or looked their way. In nearly every case, the accused claimed to be innocent of witchcraft. Some said that the girls were only inventing stories and pretending to be hurt. "Oh! You are liars," Dorcas Hoar told the afflicted girls during her hearing. "God will stop the mouths of liars." When the magistrate tried to silence her she insisted, "I will speak the truth as long as I live."[19]

The accused witches gained nothing by pleading innocence. The magistrates had no sympathy. They believed that the suspects were simply hiding their guilt. The jails filled, and the avalanche gathered power.

Chapter 5

In early New England, most people saw their ministers as protectors of the common good. During the witchcraft crisis, however, many ministers seemed to turn against the people of their own congregations. Looking back in 1700, Robert Calef wrote that "[ministers were guilty], under the mask of zeal for God, [of] branding one another with the odious name of witch [and causing] brother to accuse and prosecute brother, children their parents, and pastors and teachers their flock unto death. Shepherds had become wolves."[1]

A Special Court

Sir William Phips reached Boston in May 1692, ready to begin his duties as royal governor. He learned of the witchcraft crisis almost as soon as he stepped ashore. "I found this province miserably harassed with a most horrible witchcraft or possession of devils which had broke in upon several towns," he wrote later. "Some scores of poor people were taken with preternatural torments, some scalded with brimstone, some had pins stuck in their flesh, others hurried into the fire and water and some [were] dragged out of their houses and carried over the tops of trees and hills for many miles together."[2]

Twenty-two people had been accused of witchcraft in April. Thirty-nine more suspects were imprisoned in May.[3] The jails in Boston, Salem, and Ipswich were over-flowing. A judge and jury had to try each of the accused witches. The courts of the colony could not handle such a flood of cases. Until the governor arrived, no one knew what to do.

As a former sea captain and soldier, Phips was used to making quick decisions. Now he took immediate action. He appointed a special court called a Court of Oyer and Terminer. The terms *oyer* and *terminer* comes from French words meaning "to hear and decide." By English tradition, such courts could be appointed in haste during times of crisis. Phips later wrote that "the loud cries and clamors of the friends of the afflicted people" pressured him to appoint the court.[4] Thomas Putnam and his supporters wanted to see justice served.

On May 27, 1692, Phips called for forty jurors. All of the jurors were men. Phips also appointed nine judges to rule in the upcoming trials. Among them were John Hathorne, Jonathan Corwin, Samuel Sewall, and Bartholomew Gedney, each of whom had presided over some of the Salem hearings. The chief judge was William Stoughton, a longtime friend of Increase Mather and Cotton Mather. Stoughton had studied for the ministry, but instead had gone into politics and law. He was edu-cated and highly respected. However, he tended to be rigid and righteous. Once his mind was made up, he did not listen to arguments.[5]

All of the evidence gathered at the hearings and other investigations was used in the witchcraft trials. The defendants had no lawyers to speak for them. However, each accused person was allowed to testify on his or her own behalf. The defendants could also call witnesses who they thought would speak in their favor. The judges questioned the defendants and the witnesses. They gave instructions to the jury. The jury heard the evidence and decided if a defendant was guilty or innocent. If the jury found the accused guilty, the judges passed the sentence. Witchcraft was a capital crime under English law, and New England courts followed English law. Anyone found guilty of practicing witchcraft could be put to death.

The judges thought carefully about the evidence that would be accepted in court. They read scholarly works about witchcraft. One of these was a book by

William Stoughton was known to be a strict judge when it came to witchcraft.

Cotton Mather, *Memorable Providences.* Mather's book described in detail the case of the afflicted Goodwin children. This case, tried four years earlier in Boston, had sent the Widow Glover to the gallows.

From the beginning, the judges agreed that the discovery of a wart or mole was important evidence against a suspect. Any such mark suggested that the suspect had a familiar. Another type of evidence to be used was referred to as "mischief following anger." If a neighbor quarreled with the accused and suffered misfortune shortly afterwards, this was a sign of witchcraft.

The hardest question facing the judges was the use of spectral evidence. How could anyone prove that it was really the specter of the accused who tormented the afflicted? Suppose the devil could appear in the form of an innocent person? If this were possible, then the devil might torment people while disguised as a person who was completely blameless. After struggling with this difficult issue, the judges concluded "the devil could not assume the shape of an innocent person in doing mischief to mankind."[6] Satan could only take a person's shape, they decided, if that person allowed it to happen. Armed with this conclusion, the judges were ready to believe whatever the afflicted said in court about their spectral tormentors.

The Road to Gallows Hill

At the end of May, the judges ordered nine suspects to be moved from Boston to the jail in Salem Town. The Court of Oyer and Terminer was held in the Town House, one of Salem Town's most imposing buildings. The first nine suspects to be tried were John and Elizabeth Proctor, Susanna Martin, Alice Parker, Rebecca Nurse, Bridget Bishop, John Willard, Sarah Good, and Tituba. (Sarah Osborne had died in jail of natural causes.) All except Tituba swore that they were innocent. Because she had confessed, Tituba was kept apart from the others. The judges hoped she would give evidence against her fellow witches and wizards.

On June 2, Bridget Bishop was led to the courtroom. Spectators crowded the streets to see her pass by. When she glanced toward the empty meetinghouse, a great crash was heard from inside. Cotton Mather described the incident: "the people, at the noise, running in, found a board, which was strongly fastened with several nails, transported into another quarter of the house."[7] The villagers believed that, by some dreadful demonic power, Bridget Bishop had torn the board loose and made it fall.

For years, neighbors had suspected Bridget Bishop of practicing witchcraft. She had even been tried and acquitted twelve years before. She often quarreled with her neighbors, and she had few friends in the town.

Now an indictment claimed that Bridget Bishop "hurt, tortured, afflicted, pined, consumed, wasted and tormented" Mercy Lewis, Ann Putnam, Jr., Abigail Williams, Elizabeth Hubbard, and Mary Walcott.[8] Just as they had at the hearings, the girls shrieked and moaned when Bishop looked at them. They fell to the floor of the courtroom, twitching and writhing as if they were in

Sometimes suspected witches' bodies were inspected during the trials. People thought that if a person had certain markings on his or her body, then he or she was a witch.

agony. According to Cotton Mather, "There was little [need] to prove the witchcraft, it being evident and notorious to all beholders."[9]

Next, the court heard the testimony of persons who had long suspected Bridget Bishop of being a witch. Ten Salem Village neighbors told stories of her devilish mischief. A farmer named William Stacey reported that his cart had collapsed for no apparent reason as he passed Bridget Bishop on the road. A dyer and hatmaker, Samuel Shattuck, explained that twelve years ago Bridget Bishop had quarreled with his wife. Shortly afterward, his four-year-old son Samuel, Jr., had seizures. As time passed, Shattuck said, the boy's "understanding decayed, and ever since he has been stupefied and void of reason."[10] Doctors told him that his son had been bewitched.

One of the strangest tales came from a builder named John Bly. He swore that seven years before, in 1685, he and his fifteen-year-old son were hired to "take down the cellar wall of the old house she formerly lived in." Hidden in a crack, they found "several poppets made up of rags and hogs' bristles with headless pins in them with the points outward."[11] To John Bly and the Court of Oyer and Terminer, these poppets, or dolls, had a sinister meaning. Perhaps Bridget Bishop tortured her victims by sticking the dolls with pins.

To a modern audience, the testimony against Bridget Bishop might seem ridiculous. The stories sound to modern ears like a parade of nightmares, fantasies, and lies. But to the people of Salem Village in 1692, witchcraft was a frightening reality. For months, their neighbors and relatives seemed to have been afflicted. By now, few questioned the stories about Bridget Bishop and her evil powers. It seemed clear that she was in league with Satan.

At the close of the testimony against her, Bridget Bishop was given the chance to speak. Again, she declared that she was innocent, but she could not argue against the charges. The jury left the courtroom to make its decision. The jurors may have gathered in a room in Judge Corwin's house for privacy. In less than an hour, they returned to the courtroom with their verdict. They found Bridget Bishop guilty of practicing witchcraft. The judges sentenced her to death by hanging.

On June 10, 1692, Bridget Bishop was put in a horse-drawn cart. Once more, people lined the streets as the cart clattered beyond the edge of the village. The cart stopped at a steep rocky hill, and Bridget stepped down. Flanked by guards, jeered by the spectators, she mounted the hill and climbed the steps to the gallows platform. As the judges had ordered, she was hanged until she was dead. Her body was buried in an unmarked grave on the hillside. To this day, the hill where Bridget Bishop and most of the other condemned witches died is known as Gallows Hill.

"Speedy and Vigorous Prosecution"

Two days after Bridget Bishop's execution, Judge Nathaniel Saltonstall resigned from the Court of Oyer and Terminer. As one observer wrote later, "[Judge Saltonstall] has left the court, and is very much dissatisfied with the proceedings of it."[12] Saltonstall was not alone in his concerns. Many ordinary people, from humble farmers to merchants and ministers, were dismayed by the outcry against witches. As more and more people were arrested, the situation seemed to be out of control. Yet it was dangerous to challenge the afflicted girls. John Proctor had dared to doubt them. Now he sat in Boston Jail, awaiting trial for witchcraft.

Governor Phips had acted quickly in appointing the Court of Oyer and Terminer. Now he wondered if the court was being conducted properly. Phips sought advice from leading ministers in Boston and northeastern Massachusetts. Fifteen ministers, led by Cotton Mather, prepared a document called "The Return of Several Ministers Consulted." Throughout most of the document, the ministers called for caution. They urged that cases should be tried in a quiet atmosphere, free from the howls of afflicted persons. Finally, they questioned the value of spectral evidence: "A Demon may, . . . appear even to ill purposes, in the shape of an innocent, yea, a virtuous man."[13] This call for caution might have

Deception in the Courtroom

On at least two occasions, the afflicted persons were caught lying. Sarah Bibber accused Rebecca Nurse of stabbing and pricking her. Several of the spectators saw her pull pins from her dress and prick herself to make visible marks. In another instance, one of the accusers showed the judges a broken knife blade and claimed that Sarah Good had thrown it at her. A man in the audience came forward and explained that he had discarded that broken blade the day before. He even showed the remaining piece, which fit exactly. In both of these cases, the judges simply warned the afflicted not to lie and accepted the rest of their testimony.

slowed the momentum of the accusations and trials. Cotton Mather, however, had the final word. At the end of "The Return" he urged, "the speedy and vigorous prosecution of such as have rendered themselves obnoxious according to the direction given in the laws of God and the wholesome statutes of the English nation."[14] The "speedy and vigorous" prosecution of those who had "rendered themselves obnoxious" required all the evidence available. The court continued to rely on spectral evidence and the behavior of the accusers.

The beginning of the trials brought a new wave of witchcraft accusations. The judges could scarcely keep up with the flood of hearings. Meanwhile, the Court of Oyer and Terminer moved forward with the trials of those who waited in prison. In late June the court heard the cases of Sarah Good, Sarah Wildes, Elizabeth How, and Susanna Martin. As usual, the accusers sat in the courtroom, shrieking and writhing. Their displays were accepted as proof of the witches' evil mischief. In addition, a parade of neighbors testified about stampeding cattle, hogs taken sick, and babies who mysteriously became ill. All four women were found guilty and sentenced to die.

The case of Rebecca Nurse, however, was not decided so easily. Nurse was deeply loved by her large family. Her gentleness and piety had won her wide respect in Salem. Before the trial, thirty-nine villagers and townspeople signed a petition that read, "We never had any cause or grounds to suspect her of any such thing as she is now accused of."[15] Among those who signed were the powerful merchant Israel Porter and several of his friends. Surprisingly, since Ann Putnam, Jr., was one of her accusers, two of Thomas Putnam's uncles also signed in Rebecca Nurse's defense. The jury found Rebecca Nurse not guilty.

The moment the jury's verdict was read, the afflicted girls fell into violent fits. Their screams and wails pierced the courthouse walls. People outside began to cry and moan in sympathy. Judge Stoughton asked the jury to reconsider its decision. He reminded the jurors of a comment Nurse made when Deliverance and Abigail Hobbs, fellow prisoners, were brought to testify against her. At the sight of the Hobbs women, Nurse had exclaimed, "What! Do these persons give evidence against me now, they used to come among us?"[16] The judges asked Nurse to explain what she meant. Did she mean that she, Deliverance, and Abigail had been witches together?

This is thought to be the site once known in Salem as Gallows Hill.

Rebecca Nurse was seventy-one years old and hard of hearing. Over the din in the courtroom, she did not hear the judge's question. When she said nothing in her own defense, the jury changed its verdict to guilty.

On July 21, the five condemned witches were taken through the streets to Gallows Hill. To the end, they all declared their innocence. Most spoke humbly, in keeping with a lifetime of Puritan training. But Sarah Good, the woman who once begged from door to door, was defiant to the end. When Reverend Nicholas Noyes, pastor of the Salem Town church, urged her to confess, she cried, "You are a liar! I am no more a witch than you are a wizard, and if you take away my life God will give you blood to drink."[17]

The hanging of Rebecca Nurse seemed to prove that anyone might be a witch, and any witch would be punished. Yet an even greater challenge awaited the court and the accusers. In Boston Jail sat George Burroughs, once the pastor of the Salem Village church.

Chapter 6

"When a whole people abandons the solid ground of common sense, . . . and lets loose its passions without restraint, . . . it becomes more destructive and disastrous, . . . than tornado, conflagration, or earthquake."[1]

> —Historian Charles W. Upham in 1867; Upham's book on the witchcraft crisis, *Salem Witchcraft*, shows how mindless fear took control of eastern Massachusetts, with disastrous results.

Firebrands of Hell

On August 5, 1692, six more witchcraft suspects stood trial in Salem Town. They were John and Elizabeth Proctor, John Willard, George Jacobs, Martha Carrier, and George Burroughs. George Jacobs was accused by his own granddaughter, sixteen-year-old Margaret Jacobs, who was in jail herself. She awaited her own witchcraft trial when she made her accusations. She recanted shortly afterward, and pleaded that she had made her accusations under pressure. Martha Carrier, too, was accused by her own family. Her two teenage sons claimed that she was a witch and had forced them to join her in witchcraft. They made their accusations after they had been tied "head to heels" for hours.

The trial of George Burroughs stirred a special brew of dread and fascination among the spectators. He was a small, slight man, but he possessed amazing physical strength. During the trial, his strength was used as evidence against him. Witnesses described how, with one hand,

Burroughs could lift a heavy long-barreled gun. Once he had carried a keg full of cider from his boat to the shore, simply by putting his fingers through a large hole in its side. Such feats were proof, the judges concluded, that Burroughs had the devil's help.

All six of the suspects were found guilty and sentenced to die. Their execution date was set for August 19. Elizabeth Proctor, however, was granted a

T. H. Matteson painted *The Trial of George Jacobs, August 5, 1692.*

reprieve because she was pregnant. The judges felt that it would be wrong to destroy her unborn child. They decided to let her live until she gave birth.

On the execution day, the crowd of spectators was larger and more excited than usual. Even Cotton Mather came all the way from Boston to watch the hangings. George Burroughs was the first to meet his end. As he mounted the ladder to the gallows, he paused to pray aloud. Spellbound, the spectators listened as he recited the Lord's Prayer. It was widely believed that a witch or wizard could not say the Lord's Prayer without stumbling over the words. Yet Burroughs's voice was firm and clear. He spoke the familiar words without a single mistake. Many of the spectators were deeply shaken, and some were moved to tears. Some wondered if an innocent man was being sent to his death.

His prayer complete, Burroughs stepped to the gallows platform. As his body plunged to the end of the rope, Cotton Mather rode forward on his horse. In his ringing preacher's voice he addressed the spectators. Mather seemed eager to assure his listeners of Burroughs's guilt. He pointed out that Burroughs was not a properly ordained minister. Further, he reminded his listeners that the devil could sometimes appear as "an angel of light."[2] When Mather finished his speech, the executions went on as planned. An eyewitness named

The Reverend George Burroughs stunned the crowds in Salem by saying the Lord's Prayer perfectly before he was hanged.

Thomas Brattle wrote that all of the condemned persons died proudly:

> With great [emotion] they entreated Mr. Cotton
> Mather to pray with them: they prayed that
> God would discover what witchcrafts were
> among us; they forgave their accusers; they spake
> without reflection on jury and judges, for bring-
> ing them in guilty and condemning them:
> . . . and seemed to be very sincere, upright and
> sensible of their circumstances on all accounts.[3]

The jails were still bursting with suspects. The next trials were held on September 9. Martha Corey, Mary Easty, Alice Parker, Ann Pudeator, Dorcas Hoar, and Mary Bradbury were all found guilty and sentenced to be hanged. On September 17, nine more people received the death sentence: Margaret Scott, Wilmot Redd, Samuel Wardwell, Mary Parker (no relation to Alice), Abigail Faulkner, Rebecca Eames, Mary Lacy, Ann Foster, and Abigail Hobbs.

A few days before her execution, Mary Easty, a sister of Rebecca Nurse and Sarah Cloyce, wrote a letter to Governor Phips and the judges. She implored the judges to question the truthfulness of the afflicted persons, and to spare more innocent people from the hangman.

"I petition to Your Honors not for my own life, for I know I must die and my appointed time is set," she wrote:

> I question not that Your Honors do to the utmost of your powers in the discovery and detecting of witchcraft and witches, and would not be guilty of innocent blood for the world; but by my own innocence I know you are in the wrong way. . . . I would humbly beg of you that Your Honors would be pleased to examine these afflicted persons strictly, and keep them apart some time. . . . I beg Your Honors not to deny this, my humble petition from a poor dying innocent person, and I question not but that the Lord will give a blessing to your endeavors.[4]

Mary Easty was hanged on September 22. Martha Corey, Alice Parker, Mary Parker, Ann Pudeator, Margaret Scott, Wilmot Redd, and Samuel Wardwell all went with her to the gallows. Among the spectators was the Reverend Nicholas Noyes. As he surveyed the bodies he remarked, "What a sad thing it is to see eight firebrands of hell hanging there."[5]

The Man Who Refused to Speak

A few days before the executions of Mary Easty, Martha Corey, and the others, eighty-year-old Giles Corey was led from prison into the courtroom. When the judges asked if he would plead innocent or guilty of witchcraft, Corey refused to speak. No amount of cajoling or threatening could make him give an answer. At last the judges sent him back to his jail cell.

In March, Giles Corey had testified against his wife Martha, and his evidence helped send her to the gallows. Now, facing his own witchcraft trial, he flatly refused to take part in the judicial process. Unless he pled guilty or innocent, no trial could take place. Historians have long pondered why Giles Corey chose to take this stand. Some believe that he wanted to protect his property for his daughters and sons-in-law. If he were found guilty, the town could confiscate his livestock and other belongings. However, while he sat in jail Corey had already handed over his property to his heirs. By the time he stood before the judges he had nothing that could be taken from him but his life.

Perhaps, as some historians suggest, Giles Corey was outraged by the injustice of the trials and decided he would not take part. He knew he would be found guilty, whether he pled innocent or not. Thus far the Court of Oyer and Terminer had found every suspect guilty, and sentenced every person who did not confess to die. Corey may have hoped to lodge a protest by remaining silent in the courtroom.

When it was clear that Corey would not cooperate, the judges turned to a horrifying tactic. According to English law, a witness could be forced to testify by pressing. Heavy weights were placed on the person's chest until she or he relented. Before 1692, pressing had never been used on a witness in New England. Fortunately, after the case of Giles Corey, it was never used again.

On September 17, guards led Corey into an open field. They forced him to lie on his back and piled heavy stones on his chest. As the day wore on and Corey still refused to answer, more stones were added. Corey's ribs cracked and shattered under the crushing pressure. According to legend, he endured the ordeal with amazing courage. The torture destroyed his body, but it failed to break his spirit. To his dying breath he never declared his guilt or innocence of the witchcraft charges. He only gasped, "More weight! More weight!"[6]

Voices of Reason

The summer days of 1692 grew shorter, and at night there was a chill in the air. In any other year the people of Salem Village and the nearby towns would have been busy tending their crops and preparing for the autumn harvest. This year, however, hoes and sickles were almost forgotten. Fear and disorder held the upper hand.

Despite all the arrests and hangings, Ann Putnam, Jr., Mary Walcott, Susanna Sheldon, and the other afflicted girls were still being tormented. They claimed that hundreds of witches remained at large. As the weeks passed, the girls cried out about witches from Andover, Ipswich, Salem, and Boston. They claimed that witches came from some of the most prominent families in New England. They pointed their accusing fingers at Mrs. Thatcher, the mother-in-law of magistrate Jonathan Corwin. They cried out about two sons of Simon Bradstreet, the former governor of Massachusetts. They even accused Lady Phips, the wife of Governor William Phips, of being a witch.

In October, Governor Phips returned to Mass-achusetts after months of fighting the French and American Indians in Maine. The Court of Oyer and Terminer was supposed to handle the witchcraft crisis. But the crisis had not abated in his absence. In fact, it had risen to a pitch of delirium. Phips found one hundred fifty suspected witches crammed into the jails and some two hundred more people accused, including Lady Phips herself.

When Governor Phips returned, a new book by Cotton Mather had just been published in Boston. *Wonders of the Invisible World* described the trials of the summer and warned of the devil's conspiracy to build his kingdom in New England. The book contended that the

"The Ballad of Giles Corey"

The tale of Giles Corey captured the American imagination. In poems, stories, and plays he has been portrayed as a hero who took a stand against injustice. In "The Ballad of Giles Corey," an unknown nineteenth-century poet told the story:

> "Giles Corey," said the magistrate,
> "What have thou here to plead
> To these who now accuse thy soul
> Of crimes and horrid deed?"
>
> Giles Corey—he said not a word,
> No single word spoke he.
> "Giles Corey," said the magistrate,
>
> "We'll press it out of thee."[7]

Giles Corey was pressed to death under the weight of heavy stones.

trials and executions in Salem had been fully justified. In fact, much more work remained to be done before New Englanders would be safe.

Cotton Mather, however, was not the only person in Massachusetts who wrote about the witch trials. An anonymous pamphlet harshly criticized the judges. (Some historians think it was written by Boston minister Samuel Willard.) It described the accusing girls as "scandalous persons, liars, and loose in their conversation."[8] Another pamphlet that appeared in the Boston bookstalls was called *Cases of Conscience Concerning Evil Spirits Personating Men.* Its author was none other than the Reverend Increase Mather, Cotton Mather's own father. From the beginning, Increase Mather had not taken his son's hard line against witchcraft. In *Cases of Conscience,* he made a strong argument against spectral evidence. He stated that the devil can work his mischief while he takes the shape of a completely innocent person. "It were better that ten suspected witches should escape," he wrote, "than that one innocent person should be condemned."[9]

Feelings in Massachusetts started to change, and Increase Mather's pamphlet fit the colony's new mood. Many people found it hard to believe that a witch could have uttered George Burroughs's prayer from the gallows or written Mary Easty's letter to the judges. Then there was the fate of Giles Corey, crushed to death beneath a pile of stones. Perhaps the hunt for witches had gone

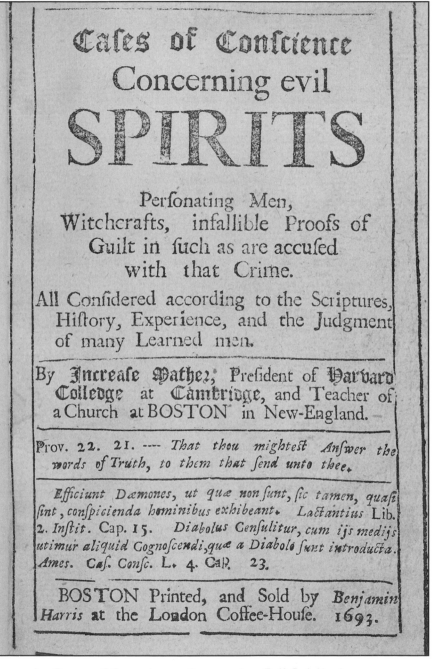

Cases of Conscience
Concerning evil
SPIRITS

Perfonating Men,
Witchcrafts, infallible Proofs of
Guilt in fuch as are accufed
with that Crime.

All Confidered according to the Scriptures,
Hiftory, Experience, and the Judgment
of many Learned men.

By *Increafe Mather,* Prefident of *Harvard
Colledge* at *Cambridge,* and Teacher of
a Church at BOSTON in New-England.

Prov. 22. 21. ---- *That thou mighteft Anfwer the
words of Truth, to them that fend unto thee.*

*Efficiunt Dæmones, ut quæ non funt, fic tamen, quafi
fint, confpicienda hominibus exhibeant.* Lactantius Lib.
2. Inftit. Cap. 15. *Diabolus Cenfulitur, cum ijs medijs
utimur aliquid Cognofcendi, quæ a Diabolo funt introducta.*
Ames. Caf. Confc. L. 4. Cap. 23.

BOSTON Printed, and Sold by *Benjamin
Harris* at the London Coffee-Houfe. 1693.

In *Cases of Conscience Concerning Evil Spirits,* Increase
Mather argued against the use of spectral evidence.

too far. Perhaps, as Increase Mather warned, innocent persons had been condemned.

On October 24, a group of Andover citizens handed a letter of protest to the judges. Their letter called for an end to witchcraft accusations and trials. "We know no one who can think himself safe," it stated, "if the accusations of children and others who are under diabolical influence shall be received against persons of good fame."[10] Meanwhile, desperate families were asking for the release of their imprisoned relatives. Many pleaded before the magistrates. Some went all the way to the governor. They spoke of children crying for their jailed mothers, beloved grandmothers starving in chains, and daughters and sons wasting away in miserable cells.

Governor Phips saw that the witchcraft crisis had had disastrous effects on the people of northeastern Massachusetts. News of the crisis was making its way back to the king in London. Phips was anxious to appear in the best possible light. Over the protests of Judge William Stoughton and his supporters, the governor again took action. On October 29, he disbanded the Court of Oyer and Terminer. Quietly, without fanfare, the Salem Witch Trials were at an end.

A Sober Aftermath

Though the Court of Oyer and Terminer had been dissolved, something had to be done about the accused

In the nineteenth century, artists often dramatized the Salem witchcraft trials. In this engraving, a witch wields her power. In reality, none of the men and women accused were really witches.

witches who still awaited trial. Governor Phips called for a special session of the Superior Court of Judicature. Judge Stoughton presided, as he had at the Court of Oyer and Terminer. But the rules had changed. The court could no longer accept spectral evidence against the accused. The visions of the afflicted girls carried no weight, and their tales of shapes that pinched and pricked were brushed aside. The court found no reason to convict the vast majority of the remaining suspects. Nearly all of the persons who declared their innocence were acquitted.

Judge Stoughton followed the new rules, but he was not happy with the outcome. He was still determined to free the colonies from the devil's hand. In January 1693, he gave the death sentence to five who had been convicted in September. He also sentenced to death three women who had confessed to practicing witchcraft. Governor William Phips promptly reprieved all eight of those that were condemned to hang. Judge Stoughton was outraged. "We were in a way to have cleared the land of the witches!" he lamented. "The Lord be merciful to the country!"[11]

Even though they had been reprieved, or found innocent altogether, dozens of people were still locked in Massachusetts jails. They could not go home until their prison fees were paid. They owed the jailers for every scrap of moldy bread they had eaten, for the dirty heaps of straw where they had slept, and even the use of the chains that had bound them to the walls. Some families sold their livestock to pay these prison debts. A few of the accused died in jail before their families were able to pay their debts.

Now and then through the fall and into the early winter the afflicted girls cried out about another servant of the devil. Their warnings went unheeded. Public opinion had turned against them. When they shrieked, people ignored them or told them to behave properly. Within a few months Ann Putnam, Jr., Abigail Williams, Mary Walcott, and the rest stopped complaining of the devil's torments. The girls who had stirred such storms settled back to the quiet lives they had pushed aside. Most of them married, raised children, and died, leaving no further marks on the pages of history beyond the horror that transpired in Salem Village.

Chapter 7

"Samuel Sewall . . . desires to take the blame and shame of it, asking pardon of men, and especially desiring prayers that God who has an unlimited authority, would pardon that sin, and all other his sins."[1]

—Judge Samuel Sewall, January 14, 1697

Slowly, with quavering steps, the people of Salem struggled to rebuild their lives. Some, like the wife and children of George Jacobs, had lost their property to the sheriffs. Others had gone into debt to free their relatives from jail. Many of those released from prison returned home sick in body and broken in spirit. Neighbors still watched them warily, the taint of suspicion still lingering in the air due to the accusations of witchcraft.

Healing the Wounds

One of the saddest cases in the wake of the witchcraft crisis was that of little Dorcas Good, Sarah Good's daughter. Dorcas was only four years old when she was accused of witchcraft and carried off to jail. She spent the next eight months in a damp, filthy cell. Years later, her father explained that the horror of those months had shattered Dorcas's mind: "being chained in the dungeon [she] was so hardly [harshly] used and terrified that she has ever since been very chargeable [unstable], having little or no reason to govern herself."[2]

Rebecca Nurse's family mourned deeply. Her children could not forgive the Reverend Parris for his role in the witchcraft crisis that led to Rebecca's hanging. A group of Rebecca's relatives and friends refused to take Communion in Parris's church. Finally, in 1697, Parris and his family left Salem Village. Betty Parris eventually married and raised several children. Abigail Williams died when she was seventeen.[3]

Massachusetts faced many hardships in the years after the witchcraft trials. Droughts parched the fields and withered the crops. A ship from the West Indies brought yellow fever to Boston, and an epidemic swept the city. Warfare with American Indians continued in Maine and New Hampshire and threatened to spread southward.

Judge Samuel Sewall, a deeply religious man, wondered if God was punishing Massachusetts for executing innocent people. When his infant daughter died, when his son's business failed, and his wife fell ill, he worried about his role in the witchcraft trials. His judgment had taken the lives of innocent men and women. Perhaps, he thought, God was punishing him for what he had done.

In January 1697, Judge Sewall handed a letter to the pastor of his Boston church. In it he made a public apology for his role in the witchcraft trials. He asked for God's forgiveness and for the forgiveness of all those who had

Judge Samuel Sewall's apology was read in front of his church congregation in 1697.

been injured by the tragic events of 1692. Sewall rose and stood humbly before the congregation as the minister read his letter aloud.

Another step toward healing came in 1706, fourteen years after the trials and hangings. Ann Putnam, Jr., was twelve years old when she made her deadly accusations. Now she was a woman of twenty-six. She had never married and still lived with her family in the farmhouse on the western edge of the village. Now she wished to become a member of the Reverend Green's church. The church required each prospective member to make a full public confession of her or his sins. As Ann Putnam, Jr., stood at her pew, the Reverend Green read her words aloud. She confessed that as a child she had "accused several persons of a grievous crime, whereby their lives were taken away from them, whom now I have just and good reason to believe they were innocent persons." She had been deluded by Satan, she explained, and had sinned out of ignorance rather than ill will. She spoke in particular of her part in condemning Rebecca Nurse and Mary Easty. "I desire to lie in the dust, and to be humbled for it," her confession read. "[I] earnestly beg forgiveness of God, and from all those . . . whose relations were taken away or accused."[4] Ann Putnam, Jr., was received into the church as a full member of the congregation.

The House of the Seven Gables

In 1851, Salem-born writer Nathaniel Hawthorne published a novel, *The House of the Seven Gables*. The story involves a curse that haunts the family of one of the Puritan judges in the witch trials. Hawthorne was the great-great-grandson of Judge John Hathorne, who presided over the first witchcraft hearings in 1692. According to legend, Hawthorne changed the spelling of the family name to distance himself from his Puritan ancestor.

Nathaniel Hawthorne

During the 1700s, Salem Town flourished as a seaport. Many young men from Salem Village went away to sea. They returned with stories of bloodthirsty pirates, Chinese princes, and enormous beasts called elephants. The world was strangely vast and mysterious, and Salem Village began to look outward.

In 1752, Salem Village finally separated from Salem Town. It became the independent village of Danvers, Massachusetts. By changing its name, it edged a little further away from its shameful memories and reached toward better times ahead.

The Search to Understand

In 1867, Charles Upham, a Massachusetts minister and politician, published a massive two-volume work called *Salem Witchcraft.* From the brittle pages of court and church records, wills, letters, maps, and property deeds Upham pieced together the story of what happened in Salem Village in 1692. Upham spent more than thirty years researching and writing his book. To this day it is considered the classic study of the witchcraft crisis.

By Upham's time, New England Puritanism had softened. For most Americans, the belief in witches and demonic possession was a curiosity from the dusty past. Upham wrote that the people of Salem Village were driven by superstition. He also suggested that feuds between neighbors fed the witchcraft panic. Powerful families, such as the Putnams encouraged the afflicted girls to point their fingers.

During the twentieth century, historians, psychologists, and even physicians pondered the events in Salem. Many tried to explain what might have caused the strange pains and convulsions of the afflicted girls. Some researchers suggested that the girls may have been poisoned by ergot, a fungus that sometimes grows on grain. Ergot poisoning causes convulsions and hallucinations. Several outbreaks occurred in Europe during the sixteenth and seventeenth centuries, causing whole villages to act strangely for days or weeks at a time. The symptoms of Ann Putnam and the other afflicted girls resemble those of people who have eaten contaminated grain.

Other investigators claimed that the afflicted girls may have had a disease called encephalitis lethargica. Encephalitis is an infection of the brain. It is caused by a variety of viruses and bacteria, often carried by mosquitoes or horseflies. Between 1920 and 1930, about five million people contracted encephalitis lethargica in a worldwide epidemic. Patients were often extremely restless, as one doctor described:

> The patient tosses about in bed, pushes the
> blankets back, pulls them up again, sits up,
> throws himself back again in a wild sort of haste,

jumps out of bed, strikes out aimlessly, talks incoherently, clucks his tongue, and whistles— this unrest lasting for days and nights without a stop.[5]

Some patients felt they were being touched by unseen hands, or thought that insects were crawling on their skin. Others saw people and objects that were not there. Sometimes patients said they saw an unearthly, hovering light. Convulsions, paralysis of arms and legs, and temporary deafness also occurred.

Perhaps ergot poisoning or encephalitis caused the girls' strange behavior. Yet some details do not ring true. These diseases affect both males and females. Few boys or men in and around Salem claimed to be bewitched. Even more revealing, the shrieks and writhings of the afflicted could be triggered by a glance from an accused witch.

Ideas about human psychology also may explain the behavior of the afflicted girls. They lived in a climate of fear—fear of American Indian attacks, Satan, and the fires of Hell. Eventually, perhaps, the fears of a few girls swelled out of control. When they felt frightened and anxious they might have imagined witches pinching and pricking them. Other girls and young women were swept into the drama. The idea of witchcraft was as contagious as a disease. Soon the afflicted were seeing witches everywhere.

The witch-hunt in Salem could not have occurred without help from the larger community. Spectators flocked to the hearings and trials. They crowded into the courtroom much as modern audiences pack a stadium, eager to see an exciting game. The New Englanders were horrified and thrilled by the writhings of the afflicted girls. Many were caught up in the excitement and began to see spectral shapes, too.

Many community leaders encouraged the spread of the witchcraft panic. Ministers such as Samuel Parris and Nicholas Noyes fed the idea that the devil was trying to take over New England. Jonathan Corwin, William Stoughton and other judges felt it was their duty to rid the land of witches. Their attitudes heightened fears and encouraged the afflicted girls to shriek and point all the more.

Thick pieces of ergot are on this stalk of rye.

What happened at Salem Village is sometimes described as a case of group hysteria. Like a raging epidemic, panic coursed through the community. It swept aside reason and compassion. Fear, blame, and hatred seized the upper hand. Then, almost as quickly as it began, the hysteria subsided. The community righted itself and viewed the damage. As time passed, most of the villagers felt that terrible wrongs had been committed. In a few months of group madness, innocent blood had been shed.

Remembering Salem

After the turmoil died down in Salem, there were no more witchcraft trials in the English colonies. However, the phenomenon of group hysteria has never disappeared. Time and time again, something triggers a sense of panic in a town or region. Fear sets in, and enemies seem to be lurking everywhere.

In 1909, hundreds of people in New Jersey and Pennsylvania claimed to have seen a demonic figure known as the Jersey Devil. For several, days schools and businesses closed as terrified people huddled in their homes. In 1939, a radio drama called "The War of the Worlds" sparked panic in the New York area. Listeners leaped to the conclusion that aliens had landed and were attacking a small New Jersey town. During the late 1950s, people all over the United States reported sighting unidentified flying objects—UFOs. The 1990s brought a spate of reports about horrifying abductions by aliens.

In the 1960s, scientists studied an instance of group hysteria that resembled the Salem Village outbreak. Girls in a Louisiana junior high school started to have strange convulsions and fainting spells. Within a few weeks, as many as four hundred girls and several boys were affected. The children generally had these "blackout spells" when an audience was present. One investigator noted, "[The] highest incidence of attacks was on the days when there were visitors in the school making inquiries regarding the hysteria outbreak. Some of the students also had attacks at home, in church, and in the movie theater."[6]

Governments have made use of group hysteria to horrifying effect. In 1915, the Turkish government fueled ethnic hatred against Armenians, who lived in Turkey. They were branded as enemies, and millions were killed. In Germany, during the 1930s, Adolf Hitler stirred up hatred of the Jews and Gypsies. In the Holocaust that followed, the Nazis killed more than 11 million people, including 6 million Jews.

In a notorious episode, group hysteria swept the United States in the early 1950s. A series of events on the international landscape led many Americans to fear the spread of a philosophy of government called Communism. Senator Joseph McCarthy of Wisconsin fanned the nation's fears. He claimed that Communists in the entertainment business were trying to influence public opinion. He even insisted that Communist agents had slipped into the highest levels of the nation's government. McCarthy's accusations led to a modern witch-hunt, with supposed Communists taking the place of suspected witches. McCarthy created a climate of fear in which friends and colleagues hurled accusations at one another. Dozens of innocent men and women went to jail. Reputations were shattered, and great careers were destroyed.

In 1953, American audiences saw the first performance of *The Crucible*, a play by Arthur Miller. The play was based on the story of the Salem witchcraft crisis. Miller did not hold tightly to historical fact, but the play conveyed a powerful sense of the panic that engulfed Salem.

The Crucible was not only about witchcraft in Salem. McCarthy's search for Communists showed Miller that witch-hunts could occur anywhere, at any time in history. Governments can encourage accusers, and accusers can spread untold fear and destruction. At such times, even well-intentioned people give in to the madness around them. In an essay about *The Crucible*, Miller noted that, "Few of us can easily surrender our belief that society must somehow make sense. The thought that the state has lost its mind and is punishing so many innocent people is intolerable. And so the evidence has to be internally denied."[7]

On May 9, 1992, some three thousand people gathered in Danvers, Massachusetts, formerly Salem Village. Three hundred years had passed since the witchcraft

Actor Daniel Day-Lewis (center) appears in the final scene of the movie version of *The Crucible* before his character, John Proctor, is hanged for witchcraft.

panic of 1692. To mark the anniversary of this tragic episode, the town of Danvers unveiled the Salem Village Witchcraft Victims Memorial. The memorial stands across the street from the site of the Salem Village Meetinghouse. On the granite memorial wall are inscribed the words: "In memory of those innocents who died during the Salem Village witchcraft hysteria of 1692." Flanking side panels bear the names and dates

The Salem witchcraft trials memorial (top) honors those who were killed
during the paranoia that plagued the small village. At the bottom is the
memorial stone of George Burroughs.

of the nineteen women and men who were executed, the five who died in prison, and of Giles Corey, the man who died under torture.

Along with the names are the words of some of the accused as they declared their innocence. "I am an innocent person. I never had to do with witchcraft since I was born. I am a Gospel woman," is inscribed beneath the name of Martha Corey. Elizabeth How is remembered for her words, "If it was the last moment I was to live, God knows I am innocent." The words of Susannah Martin speak the final truth: "Amen, Amen. A false tongue will never make a guilty person."[8]

TIMELINE

1486—Two German monks, Heinrich Kramer and Jakob Sprenger, publish *Malleus Maleficarum*, a book on witchcraft.

1620—A religious group called the Separatists, or Pilgrims, founds the Plymouth Settlement in Massachusetts.

1628—Roger Conant founds the port of Salem.

1639—A group of Salem residents are given tracts of farmland near the Ipswich River; the community is called Salem Farms.

1647—Alice Young of Windsor, Connecticut, becomes the first person in the New England colonies to be executed for witchcraft.

1672—Salem Farms, now called Salem Village, builds its first meetinghouse.

1685—The people of Massachusetts learn that King Charles II revoked the charter which has allowed them many rights of self-government.

1689—The Reverend Samuel Parris becomes the first ordained minister to serve Salem Village. Rebels overthrow New England's royal governor, Sir Edmund Andros; Massachusetts is left with no governing leader.

1692—**January:** Betty Parris and Abigail Williams begin to have strange fits after playing a fortune-telling game at the parsonage.

February: Ann Putnam, Jr., and Elizabeth Hubbard also become afflicted with fits; the girls accuse Tituba, Sarah Good, and Sarah Osborne of tormenting them.

March: The three suspects are questioned in a public hearing in Salem Village; all three are sent to jail to await trial; the girls make more accusations, and more suspects are arrested.

April: More people, mostly girls and young women, are afflicted, and more suspected witches are arrested.

May: Sir William Phips, the new royal governor, appoints a Court of Oyer and Terminer to try the witchcraft cases.

June: Bridget Bishop is tried, found guilty, and hanged.

July: Five more condemned witches are hanged—Sarah Good, Sarah Wildes, Elizabeth How, Susanna Martin, and Rebecca Nurse.

August: John and Elizabeth Proctor, John Willard, George Jacobs, Martha Carrier, and George Burroughs are tried and found guilty; all are hanged except Elizabeth Proctor, who is spared because she is pregnant.

September: Mary Easty, Martha Corey, Alice Parker, Mary Parker, Ann Pudeator, Margaret Scott, Wilmot Redd, and Samuel Wardwell are hanged as witches; Giles Corey is pressed to death when he refuses to stand trial.

October: Governor Phips disbands the Court of Oyer and Terminer.

1693—The last witchcraft suspects are released from Massachusetts jails.

1697—Judge Samuel Sewall makes a public apology for his role in the witchcraft trials.

1706—Ann Putnam, Jr., makes a public apology for helping to send innocent people to their deaths; she says she was under a delusion from Satan.

1752—Salem Village becomes the independent town of Danvers, Massachusetts.

1953—Arthur Miller's play *The Crucible* uses the Salem witchcraft hysteria as a means to look at the anti-Communist hearings led by Senator Joseph McCarthy.

1992—The Salem Village Witchcraft Victims Memorial is unveiled in Danvers.

Chapter Notes

Chapter One. Fortunes in a Glass

1. Marilynne K. Roach, *The Salem Witch Trials: A Day-by-Day Chronicle of a Community Under Siege* (Lanham, Md.: Taylor Trade Publishing, 2004), p. xxxv.

2. Peter Charles Hoffer, *The Devil's Disciples: The Makers of the Salem Witch Trials* (Baltimore: Johns Hopkins University Press, 1996), p. 2.

3. Paul Boyer and Stephen Nissenbaum, *Salem Possessed: The Social Origins of Witchcraft* (Cambridge, Mass.: Harvard University Press, 1974), p. 1.

4. Roach, p. xlvii.

5. Frances Hill, *A Delusion of Satan: The Full Story of the Salem Witch Trials* (New York: da Capo, 1995), p. 14.

6. Roach, p. 18.

7. Hoffer, p. 68.

8. Hill, p. 25.

9. Roach, p. 21.

Chapter Two. A Dreadful World Unseen

1. "The Black Death: Bubonic Plague," The Middle Ages.net, 2008, <www.themiddleages.net/plague.html> (May 6, 2008).

2. Michael H. Stone, *Healing the Mind: A History of Psychiatry from Antiquity to the Present* (New York: W. W. Norton, 1997), p. 24.

3. Selma R. Williams, *Riding the Nightmare: Women and Witchcraft from Europe to Colonial Salem* (New York: Harpers Perennial, 1978), p. 35.

4. Ibid., p. 37.

5. Ibid., p. 41.

6. Ibid., p. 42.

7. Charles W. Upham, *Salem Witchcraft: With an Account of Salem Village and A History of Opinions on Witchcraft and Kindred Subjects* (Mineola, N.Y.: Dover Publications, Inc., 2000), p. 230.

8. Richard Godbeer, *Escaping Salem: The Other Witch Hunt of 1692* (New York: Oxford University Press, 2005), p. 99.

9. Ibid., p. 234.

10. Anne Llewelyn Barstow, *Witchcraze* (New York: HarperOne, 1954), p. 23.

11. Alice Morse Earle, *Home Life in Colonial Days* (Stockbridge, Mass.: The Berkshire Travelers Press, 1974), p. 71.

12. Michael Tougias, "King Philip's War in New England," *The History Place Special Presentation*, 1997, <http://www.historyplace.com/specials/kingphilip.htm> (May 6, 2008).

13. Frances Hill, *A Delusion of Satan: The Full Story of the Salem Witch Trials* (New York: da Capo, 1995), p. 10.

14. John Putnam Demos, *Entertaining Satan: Witchcraft and the Culture of Early New England* (New York: Oxford University Press, 1982), p. 11.

15. Laurie Winn Carlson, *A Fever in Salem: A New Interpretation of the New England Witch Trials* (Chicago: Ivan R. Dee, 1999), pp. 17–18.

16. Hill, p. 73.

17. Upham, p. 304.

Chapter Three. Fertile Ground

1. Paul Boyer and Stephen Nissenbaum, *Salem Possessed: The Social Origins of Witchcraft* (Cambridge, Mass.: Harvard University Press, 1974), p. 45.

2. Ibid., p. 40.

3. Ibid., p. 92.

4. Ibid., p. 41.

5. Ibid., p. 41.

6. Marilynne K. Roach, *The Salem Witch Trials: A Day-by-Day Chronicle of a Community Under Siege* (Lanham, Md.: Taylor Trade Publishing, 2004), p. xxviii.

7. Boyer and Nissenbaum, p. 119.

8. Charles W. Upham, *Salem Witchcraft: With an Account of Salem Village and A History of Opinions on Witchcraft and Kindred Subjects* (Mineola, N.Y.: Dover Publications, Inc., 2000), p. 197.

9. Roach, p. xliv.

10. Marion L. Starkey, *The Devil in Massachusetts: A Modern Enquiry into the Salem Witch Trials* (New York: Doubleday, 1989), pp. 129–130.

11. Ibid., p. 133.

12. Ibid., p. 133.

13. Ibid., p. 135.

Chapter Four. Torments and Trials

1. Frances Hill, *A Delusion of Satan: The Full Story of the Salem Witch Trials* (New York: da Capo, 1995), p. 48.

2. Ibid., p. 43.

3. Ibid., p. 44.

4. Ibid., p. 17.

5. Mary Beth Norton, *In the Devil's Snare: The Salem Witchcraft Crisis of 1692* (New York: Alfred A. Knopf, 2002), p. 28.

6. Ibid., p. 44.

7. Marilynne K. Roach, *The Salem Witch Trials: A Day-by-Day Chronicle of a Community Under Siege* (Lanham, Md.: Taylor Trade Publishing, 2004), p. 60.

8. Hill, p. 89.

9. Norton, p. 60.

10. Roach, p. 93.

11. Ibid., p. 29.

12. Norton, p. 53.

13. Ibid., p. 71.

14. Roach, p. 66.

15. Hill, p. 102.

16. Roach, p. 80.

17. Ibid., p. 101.

18. Charles W. Upham, *Salem Witchcraft: With an Account of Salem Village and A History of Opinions on Witchcraft and Kindred Subjects* (Mineola, N.Y.: Dover Publications, Inc., 2000), p. 419.

19. Roach, p. 105.

Chapter Five. Shepherds Into Wolves

1. Charles W. Upham, *Salem Witchcraft: With an Account of Salem Village and A History of Opinions on Witchcraft and Kindred Subjects* (Mineola, N.Y.: Dover Publications, Inc., 2000), p. xiv.

2. Frances Hill, *A Delusion of Satan: The Full Story of the Salem Witch Trials* (New York: da Capo, 1995), p. 154.

3. Paul Boyer and Stephen Nissenbaum, *Salem Possessed: The Social Origins of Witchcraft* (Cambridge, Mass.: Harvard University Press, 1974), p. 31.

4. Ibid., pp. 154–155.

5. Mary Beth Norton, *In the Devil's Snare: The Salem Witchcraft Crisis of 1692* (New York: Alfred A. Knopf, 2002), p. 198.

6. Marion L. Starkey, *The Devil in Massachusetts: A Modern Enquiry into the Salem Witch Trials* (New York: Doubleday, 1989), p. 53.

7. Upham, p. 487.

8. Hill, p. 162.

9. Norton, p. 206.

10. Marilynne K. Roach, *The Salem Witch Trials: A Day-by-Day Chronicle of a Community Under Siege* (Lanham, Md.: Taylor Trade Publishing, 2004), p. 159.

11. Ibid., p. 207.

12. Hill, p. 198.

13. Roach, p. 171.

14. Ibid., p. 172.

15. Hill, p. 156.

16. Peter Charles Hoffer, *The Devil's Disciples: The Makers of the Salem Witch Trials* (Baltimore: Johns Hopkins University Press, 1996), p. 161.

17. Roach, p. 202.

Chapter Six. Innocent Blood

1. Charles W. Upham, *Salem Witchcraft: With an Account of Salem Village and A History of Opinions on Witchcraft and Kindred Subjects* (Mineola, N.Y.: Dover Publications, Inc., 2000), p. 313.

2. Frances Hill, *A Delusion of Satan: The Full Story of the Salem Witch Trials* (New York: da Capo, 1995), p. 179.

3. Ibid.

4. Peter Charles Hoffer, *The Devil's Disciples: The Makers of the Salem Witch Trials* (Baltimore: Johns Hopkins University Press, 1996), pp. 164–165.

5. Hill, p. 188.

6. Marilynne K. Roach, *The Salem Witch Trials: A Day-by-Day Chronicle of a Community Under Siege* (Lanham, Md.: Taylor Trade Publishing, 2004), p. 297.

7. Frances Hill, ed., *The Salem Witch Trials Reader* (New York: da Capo, 2000), p. 81.

8. Hill, *A Delusion of Satan*, p. 185.

9. Roach, p. 309.

10. Marion L. Starkey, *The Devil in Massachusetts: A Modern Enquiry into the Salem Witch Trials* (New York: Doubleday, 1989), p. 220.

11. Ibid., p. 229.

Chapter Seven. A Legacy of Questions

1. Richard Francis, *Judge Sewall's Apology: The Salem Witch Trials and the Forming of an American Conscience* (New York: HarperCollins, 2005), pp. 181–182.

2. Peter Charles Hoffer, *The Devil's Disciples: The Makers of the Salem Witch Trials* (Baltimore: Johns Hopkins University Press, 1996), p. xi.

3. Marilynne K. Roach, *The Salem Witch Trials: A Day-by-Day Chronicle of a Community Under Siege* (Lanham, Md.: Taylor Trade Publishing, 2004), p. 518.

4. Ibid., pp. 568–569.

5. Laurie Winn Carlson, *A Fever in Salem: A New Interpretation of the New England Witch Trials* (Chicago: Ivan R. Dee, 1999), p. 85.

6. Hans Sebald, *Witch-Children: From Salem Witch Hunts to Modern Courtrooms* (Amherst, N.Y.: Prometheus Books, 1995), p. 231.

7. Arthur Miller, "Why I Wrote the Crucible," in Frances Hill, ed., *The Salem Witch Trials Reader* (New York: da Capo, 2000), p. 388.

8. "Salem Village Witchcraft Victims' Memorial at Danvers," *Salem Witch Trials Documentary Archive and Transcription Project*, 2002, <etext.virginia.edu/salem/witchcraft/Commemoration.html> (May 6, 2008).

Glossary

afflicted—Affected by an illness or evil magic.

communion—Ceremony in many Christian churches, in which members partake of wine and bread that represents the blood and body of Jesus Christ.

conjuration—Magic.

dissemble—To lie or deceive.

encephalitis lethargica—An infection of the brain that causes agitation, paralysis, and many other symptoms.

ergot poisoning—Poisoning caused by eating grain infected with a fungus; it can cause temporary insanity.

faction—A group of people on one side of an issue.

familiar—A demon that helps a witch carry out her evil plans; it was thought to take the form of an animal.

group hysteria—Situation in which fear and panic sweep through a community.

heretic—Person who turns against an established religion or belief.

magistrate—Judge.

monotheistic religion—A religion whose followers believe in one god.

ordained minister—Minister who has been approved by the heads of an established church; an ordained minister may perform baptisms and offer communion.

parsonage—Minister's house.

piety—Intense religious feeling.

sect—A new religious group that splits off from an established religion.

selectman—Town official.

spectral evidence—Evidence based on the claim that a witch had been seen in a dream, or that a witch had been seen in spirit form.

Further Reading

Aronson, Marc. *Witch-Hunt: Mysteries of the Salem Witch Trials*. New York: Simon & Schuster, 2005.

Burgan, Michael. *The Salem Witch Trials*. Minneapolis, Minn.: Compass Point Books, 2005.

Burgan, Michael, and Brendan McConville. *Massachusetts*. Washington, D.C.: National Geographic, 2005.

Crewe, Sabrina and Michael V. Uschan. *The Salem Witch Trials*. Milwaukee, Wis.: Gareth Stevens Pub., 2005.

Dunkleberger, Amy. *A Student's Guide to Arthur Miller*. Berkeley Heights, N.J.: Enslow Publishers, Inc., 2005.

Kallen, Stuart A. *Figures of the Salem Witch Trials*. Detroit: Lucent Books/Thomson Gale, 2005.

MacBain, Jenny. *The Salem Witch Trials: A Primary Source History of the Witchcraft Trials in Salem, Massachusetts*. New York: Rosen, 2003.

Magoon, Kekla. *The Salem Witch Trials*. Edina, Minn.: ABDO Pub. Co., 2008.

Nardo, Don. *The Salem Witch Trials*. Detroit: Lucent Books, 2007.

Nelson, Sheila. *The Northern Colonies: The Quest for Freedom, 1600-1700*. Philadelphia: Mason Crest Publishers, 2005.

Roach, Marilynne K. *In the Days of the Salem Witchcraft Trials*. Boston: Houghton Mifflin, 2003.

Roberts, Russell. *Life in Colonial America*. Hockessin, Del.: Mitchell Lane Publishers, 2007

Stefoff, Rebecca. *Witches and Witchcraft*. New York: Marshall Cavendish Benchmark, 2007.

Wallis, Jeffrey. *Trials in Salem*. Boston: Hougton Mifflin, 2005.

Yolen, Jane. *The Salem Witch Trials: An Unsolved Mystery from History*. New York: Simon and Schuster, 2004.

Internet Addresses

Salem Witchcraft Hysteria
<www.nationalgeographic.com/salem.us>
This interactive site explores life during the witch hysteria.

The Salem Witchcraft Papers
<etext.virginia.edu/salem/witchcraft/texts/transcripts.html>
Includes complete transcripts of the witchcraft trials.

The Salem Witchcraft Trials of 1692
<www.law.umkc.edu/faculty/projects/ftrials/salem/SALEM.HTM>
Includes pictures, documents, articles, and maps.

INDEX